PIONEERING OUT WEST:
A MEMOIR OF EDITH BERRY

By

Elaine McKeag Nielsen

Cover Painting: "Sandhills Sunrise", by Mary Ann Anderberg, a prominent Nebraska painter, and one of Edith Berry's granddaughters

FORWARD

A few years before my Grandmother Berry crossed the Great Divide, a television crew came to town and wanted to film several generations of women from the same family. Eventually they were given my name and phone number.

"We are wondering", the voice over the phone inquired, "If it would be possible for you to locate four generations of women in your family?"

"Actually", I replied, "I suppose there are now five generations of females in my family counting the present crop of kids."

"Would it be possible to gather them into one place to be interviewed and photographed by us?" was the further inquiry.

"Well, yes, I suppose so", I replied. And so it came to pass that Grandma Berry (age, mid-nineties), my mother (mid-seventies), myself (mid-fifties), and my eldest daughter (mid-thirties) gathered in my living room to be televised one afternoon in late summer. The crew, who all seemed to be in their late twenties, were not really interested in the fifth generation, a pack of my grandchildren who kept coming in and out of the house accompanied by the odd dog or cat.

(Five Generations: Elaine McKeag Nielsen, Melody Nielsen McGowan, Elvina Berry McKeag, James McGowan, Edith Stansbery Berry)

When they turned on the lights and the microphones it soon became obvious they had a point to make: Women had come a long ways and were still On The

March. And Modern Woman (i.e. my eldest daughter) was liberated beyond the dreams of a woman like my Grandma Berry.

How little they knew, and how impossible it was to make them understand! Grandma Berry was born in 1887 here in Keith County just a month after her parents and three little sisters arrived here from eastern Nebraska. They were part of a steady influx of permanent settlers to take land in western Nebraska, which had heretofore been considered country too arid to farm. Ogallala's brief existence at the end of the Texas Trail and the center of the open range cattle trade was just ending.

Grandma's father was a blacksmith, a farmer, a hunter, and indeed anything he needed to be to support his ever growing family (eventually there were nine children). They grew up helping their father and mother in whatever project was at hand. They survived drouth and hard times of all sorts over the next few years. They moved about the county, and the houses they lived in were primitive to say the least. At last the father of the family took a contract to put up hay along the North Platte River Valley for William Paxton, one of the open range cattlemen who retained interests in the area. Paxton's hay meadows extended from the ranch headquarters at Keystone more than twenty five miles east to the Birdwood Creek.

Grandma's mother (a saint if there ever was one) accompanied the crew along with the younger members of the family to cook and care for all of them. They camped out in tents along the way for the duration of the haying season——mid-July until the end of September. The cook stove went along in a wagon to be set up at each camp so that her mother could prepare meals and heat water. And the water usually had to be carried to camp from the river.

Grandma drove the stacker team in the hayfield when she was only ten years old. By the time she was thirteen she was driving one of the horse drawn mowers. In 1897 when her father took a homestead on Lonergan Creek, Grandma and her sisters helped him build a four bedroom house. She helped plow fireguards. She cooked, sewed, gardened, canned, preserved, and always she helped with the younger children.

At eighteen she married a young Texas cowboy who worked for the ranches around Hyannis. The two of them lived in a two room sod house after they were wed, and sometimes on a Sunday they would hunt coyotes together. She rode horseback on the only saddle they owned, and her husband rode bareback.

They took a homestead of their own in Keith County just before the birth of my mother, their eldest child. Uncle John, born two years later, always claimed he was born in the buckboard with the team running away, a tale somewhat closer to fact than many he told.

Grandma learned to handle a gun, and was one of the best shots anywhere. She loved the mountains, and after being widowed in 1935, she moved to Wyoming. She lived there for twenty years in a log cabin along the banks of Canyon Creek. At sixty five she packed into the Big Horn Mountain wilderness on horseback, shot a deer, dressed it out, and packed back to her cabin. She was an avid fisherman, and one uncle opined that was why she lived so long, because as he put it, "The Lord doesn't count the time you spend fishing."

Grandma needed liberating about as much as a mountain lion in its native habitat. Hers was the timeless legacy of the many women who have been "equal to the occasion", really the only equality that counts. Never the less, the TV crew that warm August afternoon in my living room were determined to view her as somehow limited and unfulfilled. They talked to us all for two and a half hours, and really never did quite figure things out. They tried. They really did, but somehow their lack of experience in history and past times kept them from asking the right questions and coming to the correct conclusions.

Back in Lincoln those young technicians of stunted understanding and one dimensional insight edited the two and a half hours down to a five minute segment that appeared in a half hour production about the contrasts between then and now—-Grandma Berry and the New Woman, represented by several high school girl rodeo participants on the local scene and the great-granddaughter who had attended college. Poor blind leaders of the blind. In the world of TV editing it is possible to make water run up hill, and mistake pure gold for lead.

Over the years I recorded many of Grandma Berry's tales and reminiscences, and it has seemed that her experiences just might entertain and inform others as much as they have the multitude of her relatives. Herewith many of the stories she told interspersed with the recollections I have of her and the information I have been able to research about those long gone times and places.

Elaine Nielsen

TABLE OF CONTENTS

CHAPTER SYNOPSIS

I. Beginning in Keith County ... Background of how the elder Stansberys met, married, and began their family. Edith was the fourth daughter, born just a month after they moved to Keith County.

II. Hay Camp And The Claim On Lonergan...The family adventures putting up hay on the North Platte River Valley for cattleman, William Paxton. W.P. Stansbery files a homestead claim on Lonergan Creek.

III. Lonergan...The home they built on the creek, and the neighborhood along the North Platte River. School and friends.

IV. Belles and Beaus...The sisters become young women, and activities include dances, picnics, and other social gatherings.

V. The Happy Summer...Dances and social engagements. Arelias, the new cowboy from Texas, takes Edith to Paxton on the train.

VI. A Courtship Becomes Stormy...Edith resents the long absences of Arelias because of his work on the ranches in the sandhills far to the North.

VII. Ogallala, 1900...The story of Arelias Berry and his arrival in Ogallala.

VIII. Buzzard's Roost and Sandhill Cow Camps...H.B. Read and the Valley Land and Cattle Company. Edith's letter and a decision to return to Texas.

IX. A Wedding at High Noon...Edith and Arelias are married at the Stansbery home on Lonergan Creek amid friends and family.

X. A Cow Camp Bride...Edith's adventures in the cattle country living in a two room sod house, and learning about ranch life. The birth of their first child, Elvina.

XI. The Soddie On The Claim...Arelias files on a homestead near the Stansbery home. Son John is arrives unexpectedly.

XII. Texas ...Edith goes to Texas and meets Arelias's relatives and visits his homeland.

XIII. 1913...A blizzard and the new home in the valley.

XIV. John, Horses, and A Church...The many scrapes and adventures of rearing children on a ranch and driving Double X horses. Also, the organizing of the Lemoyne Church.

XV. The First Studebaker...They buy their first car. Hazards of learning to drive it, and then the adventures of a trip to Wyoming.

XVI. War And Flu ...The new bridge is built at Lemoyne, United States enters World War I, and Edith gets Spanish Influenza.

XVII. Fifteen Flat Tires to Yellowstone....A trip to Yellowstone Park after World War I becomes an ordeal of endurance on the road home.

XVIII. Elvina: The School Years...Edith goes to California to visit her parents. The many different schools Elvina and John attended.

XIX. Ruth...The child born to Edith and Arelias the summer just before Elvina's eighteenth birthday.

XX. Glad Times, Sad Times...The Stansbery parents' Golden Wedding Anniversary celebration. The deaths of the elder Stansberys. The 1931 spring blizzard, and a 1933 family reunion.

CHILDHOOD RECOLLECTIONS OF EARLY KEITH COUNTY

"Dad's full name was William Plaskett Stansbery. He grew up in south eastern Iowa along the Missouri border. His father was George Stansbery, and his mother was Susan Plaskett Stansbery. There were several brothers and sisters. Some I knew, but quite a few I never met. I never knew Grandma Susan Plaskett Stansbery because she died before my parents met and were married. The Stansbery family lived at Birmingham, Iowa, when my father and mother first met.

Mother's maiden name was Elvina Devine. She was born in West Virginia in 1858, the oldest of five children born to Jacob and Mahalia Darrah Devine. The Devines came west by covered wagon to Iowa from West Virginia. Grandpa Devine was a Baptist preacher as well as a farmer. Grandma Devine was sort of frail, and she died soon after the family arrived in Iowa. Mom was only thirteen at the time, but she managed the household and took care of the younger children until she married Dad when was twenty two years old.

Dad wrote to Mother before they were married. We kids found some of the letters years ago. One letter we found especially tickled us. In it Dad seemed to be a bit jealous, and he was pretty sarcastic over another man Mother had apparently also been dating. Dad's spelling and grammar were very original—-he always shot a lot better than he read or wrote.

It seemed Mother had visited the Stansbery family at Birmingham, Iowa, and wrote him afterwards of her safe arrival home. She also wrote that she had attended a barbecue with this other admirer when she returned home. Dad replied at once, beginning his letter "Dearest Friend", and told her he was glad for her safe arrival home. He went on to say, "...Vina, I'm glad you have been enjoying yourself since you have been home, for you had a lonesome time when you were down here. You said you went to a barbecue with a terrible good looking little fellow. That is al rite. Them is the cind for me. I like little fellows and big girls. You said your fellow was only 18 years old and you expected I would think he had better stay at home awhile with his mother. I don't think no such a thing. I think he had better go while he is young. For when he gets old, he can't. You can take him and train him to your own notion.."

Dad went on to say that he would be coming to her town soon and would take her for a buggy ride on Sunday, "...Providing you have no objections or your company isn't otherwise engaged. If not write and tell me the consequences, and if all is well, tell me where you will be..." He closed the letter asking her "...Permit me to remain your friend as ever, W.P. Stansbery." An impulsive postscript added, "Vina, write as soon as you can.." (It seemed strange to think that Mom had called him "Willy" in those days, and he had called her "Vina".) (1)

Not so long after this letter he managed to persuade Mother to become his wife. They were married March 21, 1880, in Wayne County, Iowa, by the Rev. David Peachen, whose wife and daughter acted as witnesses. Mother recorded all of this very carefully in her Bible. (2)

1

According to that same Bible the baby daughter that arrived a year later on March 25, 1881, was named Aletha. However she was always called "Letha" by all the family. Mom and Dad sometimes referred to Letha as the "Hawkeye" because she was the only one of us born in Iowa. That same year Dad rented a farm near York, Nebraska, and they moved there. Two more daughters joined the family in York—-Edna, born April 12, 1883, and Ethel, born March 11, 1885.

During the years when she was responsible for her younger brothers and sister Mother learned to be a very good nurse. She knew a lot about caring for wounds and illness, and when they were at York she saved Dad's life.

He always loaded his own ammunition, and while he was re-loading shotgun shells a primer cap went off in his hand. Blood poison set in and he nearly died, for infection of this nature was the curse of the frontier. Mom dealt with it by placing his arm over a wash boiler with the lid sloping under his arm into the boiler so that she could pour warm water over the wound and drain it into the boiler. With the help of a visiting relative she kept this up continuously for most of a day and night until the infection subsided. Often doctors on the frontier were only able to save someone's life from blood poison by amputating the limb so afflicted.

In the spring of 1886 Dad and his father traveled west to see the prairie lands near Ogallala, Nebraska, a little town along the Union Pacific Railroad where Texas cattle were trailed to be shipped east or turned on the open range there. It was still frontier country out there, and very little of the country was being homesteaded yet. The Union Pacific had a stockyard on its railroad there, and Ogallala boomed with the cattle trade for several years. However by 1886 the northern ranges were stocked and overstocked, and after a series of bad winters the bloom was off the cattle trade. Traffic up the Texas Trail dwindled to a trickle, and people began to take homestead claims to farm there.

1886 was a wet year, and Dad saw fields green with lush wheat that spring and summer. I suppose it impressed him, all right, but the abundance of wild game he saw probably influenced him more. He and my Grandad Stansbery bought a timber claim relinquishment (3) south of Ogallala before returning home.

Dad somehow managed to take a baby antelope back to York with him as a pet for the little girls. It was quite gentle and followed them all around. It liked bread and butter and Mom was quite disgusted with it for taking bread and butter away from the girls. It died before the family moved west. Wild things do not really do well as pets in a domestic situation.

Dad went out west ahead of the family and rented a house from Abe Keithley that was located near his tree claim. Newcomers were pouring into the territory that spring, so he set up a blacksmith forge, and was soon sharpening plows and discs for the other settlers. Mother and the three little girls arrived in late March that year, (1887).

Bill Draves, a neighbor who came to get a plow sharpened, saw the kids playing near the house. He asked Dad, "Who is that woman and those children up there by the house?"

Dad proudly said, "My wife and kids."

Draves retorted, " Ah, go on, you ain't old enough to have all those kids."

"You just come up and see if they don't call me 'Pappa' ", Dad laughed.

2

Besides being a blacksmith Dad was a good carpenter and builder. Like many of those who came West he could do most anything he had to, but what he liked doing best was to hunt and fish. Often that is how he put meat on the table in those early years. We children all grew up on wild meat, and it still tastes best to me.

That first home in Keith County was located southwest of Ogallala on a plain of endless grass and no trees. It was such flat and lonely country! Mom said you could see the tumble weeds roll for miles on a windy day. Many cattle and buffalo died during the hard winter of 1886, and bones littered the whole landscape. Some settlers picked up wagon loads of bones to ship back east on the railroad to sell for mineral and fertilizer.

Mother was pregnant, and a month after they moved into the Keithley house I was born, April 12, 1887.They named me Edith Ivy. I had dark hair and blue eyes, and was quite healthy, Mother said.

Unlike 1886 crops did not do as well in Keith County the summer of 1887, because there was very little rain. Dad hunted a lot, and was sometimes gone for several days at a time. Besides providing meat for his own family he killed and dressed wild game to sell to railroad workers. He would take it to the railroad on certain days, and the train stopped for it. I think the meat they bought was for their own families rather than for market, although many settlers sold wild meat for eastern markets on the frontier then. It was a source of cash in a land where cash was scarce.

One day while Dad was away hunting a cowboy galloped up and shouted at Mom that a herd of cattle was out of control and stampeding towards the river. Mom pushed a table into the corner of the kitchen, pulled the three older girls under it, and then took me in her arms and got under it also. The herd thundered over, through and around our house, but we all survived unhurt. What a shambles Mother must have had to straighten up afterwards!

We girls learned to help in any way we could when we were still very young. Letha often helped Dad in the blacksmith shop when she was only seven years old. She would pull a cord that worked the bellows up and down beside the forge while Dad heated metal and tools. She also rode a lister with Grandfather Stansbery while he planted trees to fulfill the terms of the relinquishment claim. He was planting box elder seeds, and Letha was supposed to pull the lever to drop a seed into the furrow every time a rag tied to the lister wheel came around. She said afterwards that she got very tired and sleepy before they were finished.

Many of the settlers in the neighborhood were German immigrants, and could not speak English. They built a Lutheran church near where we lived that came to be known as Trinity Lutheran. It was a prominent landmark in that lonely country and still stands, the only reckoning point still there by which one can locate where we lived so long ago.

The Burlington Railroad was building across southern Keith County the summer of 1887, and the town of Grant began along the new railroad. Until this time everyone that settled in that country had to go to Ogallala for materials and supplies. This meant crossing the South Platte River. In fact both the North and South branches of the Platte passed through the northern half of Keith County, and it was obvious that several bridges must be built in order to get to Ogallala from any where. The cost of building bridges meant increased property taxes.

Those thrifty German settlers over south didn't see any reason for paying to build bridges over the Platte, if they could trade in Grant along the Burlington Railroad. So the summer of 1887 they circulated a petition to form a new county by dividing Keith County. Grant was to be the new county seat. Dad signed the petition along with most of his neighbors. The vote in the fall favored the petition, and Perkins County was organized. When my sister, Elsie, was born on May 1, 1889, in the same house where I was born, she was born in Perkins County instead of Keith County.

Water was always a problem in that country. At first Dad hauled water in barrels from a shallow lagoon near the house. Mom always recalled seeing buffalo chips on the bottom and wishing she had another source of water. By the end of that first summer the lagoon dried up and Dad began to haul water from a neighbor's well. That well had been dug by hand, and it was nearly two hundred feet deep.

Crops failed three years in a row. In the spring of 1890 Mom begged Dad to take his wheat into the Ogallala mill to be ground into flour rather than planting it. She reasoned at least they would have bread that summer. Dad planted it though, and although it came up in late spring, the summer was hot and dry, and by the end of July the wheat died.

Dad hired a fourteen year old neighbor boy, Ted Elmshaeuser, to help him that summer, and didn't make enough to pay the boy's wages. He heard of work on the railroad in Utah, and after the wheat crop failed, he took the boy and went there to work in Utah on the railroad near Devil's Slide until he could pay what he owed and make some money for the family as well. Mom had a mighty tough time while they were gone. Mom's sister in Iowa sent her a five dollar bill, and Mom said it was the only time she could remember getting five pairs of shoes for five dollars. Each of us five little girls got a pair.

Dad decided to sell the south tableland farm when he returned from Utah. He wanted to move the family to the North Platte River Valley instead. It was different country with more wild game and water available everywhere, so he sold the farm and paid off his father. We had to move to another house then because the house we had been living in was no longer for rent. Until Dad could locate a place on the North River he rented the Wickless place on the south table still south of Ogallala. It rained the night we moved into it, and the roof leaked. Mother had a terrible time trying to keep us children dry. There was a sort of dugout or cave with dirt walls beside the house. I can still remember the earthy smell of it as we girls explored it. No matter how many trees were planted on that flat plain, few of them grew because the rains were scarce for several years. There was consequently little shade or relief from the scorching summer heat even though fall was near.

One evening while we were there Mom and Dad were going to drive to a neighbor's home after supper for something. I wanted to go along but Dad was in a hurry and Mom said, "Oh, you are too dirty to go visiting." I went out where Dad was hitching up the team and asked him if I could go. He had a large box in the wagon, and he picked me up and put me in it, saying, "Be still." When Mother came out, they drove away. I soon forgot to be still and began to sing, so Mother looked around and found me. Dad laughed, and then I must have gone to sleep, for I remember no more about the trip.

We moved many times in those years. Dad soon rented a small house from a widow, Mrs. Nona Wolf, on the North Platte River Valley, but she was still living there, and until she got her things moved we needed a place to live. R.K. Lewis was a merchant who ran a store in Ogallala, and he owned land just east of the Wolf place. There was a very small sod house on it where Lewis had lived before he opened his store. It was vacant at this time and he told Dad to move into it until Mrs. Wolf moved. Lewis had run sheep there and there were still sod pens and a small sod barn, as well as the small sod house. A little creek began up above the house and we carried water from the spring to the house.

The thing about sod houses in those days was that sometimes under the floors there were fleas. Many times I would wake to feel Mother's soft fingers hunting the vicious little vermin out of our clothes by lamplight. She would hear us fussing in our sleep, and get up to see what she could do. What a wonderful, patient, loving mother we had, and at times she had to live under very trying conditions.

We moved to the Wolf place late that spring of 1891. My sister, Eva, was born August 12, 1891. She was a small baby, and always a bit frailer than the rest of us. There were six Stansbery sisters now. I shall always remember how forlorn Elsie looked when they showed us the new baby. She was only two years old herself, and she stood by the bed in her little red flannel petticoat and felt neglected.

There were quite a few families living along the North Platte River Valley by that time, and in the fall they all decided to start a school for their children. The bachelors of the neighborhood were not in favor of this, but all the women and mothers insisted on voting on the matter along with the men, and so the vote favored the school. It was held in R.K. Lewis's little sod house that we had just moved out of. The older girls started to school that fall, and although I was only four years old at the time, Mom let me go along.

We had three months of school in the fall and then three more in the spring. It was too cold to go in the winter time. The men built a few long benches for us to sit upon, and then made some higher ones for desks. The light from the little deep-set windows typical of a sod house was dim and inadequate, but on nice days the door was left open for more sunlight. There were ten students in school that first year including us four Stansbery girls. There were also two Patrick children, three Combs, and a Peterson boy.

Our teacher was a young girl and this was her first term of school. In those days if you could pass an exam to qualify for a teaching certificate, a girl could teach school if she graduated from the eighth grade. Our teacher that first year was probably not sixteen years old. Occasionally she went to sleep during recess. Until she woke up and rang the bell we ran wild over the hills gathering rocks and arrowheads and sliding down steep sand banks.

Sometimes we went too far away to hear the bell. The boys made guns out of the hollow weed stalks around the school. They would load them with gravel for shot and sling them against the ankles of us girls. This generally caused a battle. We also played hide-and-seek in the little sod sheep pens.

One evening as we were going home from school, there were three of the Combs children with us. We saw a weasel and we all tried to kill it. Clarence Combs kicked it with his bare foot and it bit his toe. How he yelled!

We went to school in the little sod house for four years, and then they built a frame schoolhouse for us. That last fall we were in the sod school I remember one day our studies were interrupted when numerous bull snakes began sticking their heads out of holes and cracks in the walls. One snake almost slid off the top of the door frame. Next day we came prepared to kill them, and not one was to be found. Our parents decided that the snakes were denning up for winter and trying to find suitable places in the sod walls. Anyway, the next day they were all gone.

Very few of the settlers had much education. Still, in the winter sometimes the neighbors would all gather at the school house for a spelling bee. We all had a lot of fun spelling and singing. Dad was a good hunter, and in the fall when he killed the first deer or antelope, he and Mom would invite the neighbors in for a big feed. They all laughed and told hunting stories, and then generally played cards afterward. High Five was a popular card game with them.

The neighbors were all sociable and hospitable to each other. They had old time dances at different homes sometimes, and they would dance all night with a mouth harp for music. Each woman would bring something to eat when they stopped for lunch at midnight. I can remember playing while they danced, then crawling under some chair or table to sleep. They danced the old quadrilles, and these were as often called by a woman as a man. They surely had a grand time.

One evening the folks were going to a dance somewhere, and they sent Edna and I to the garden after vegetables for supper. We rode a mule, and he fell down with us in a patch of sandburs. We were so full of stickers that we had to stay home that night.

That same winter on January 22, 1895, our first baby brother was born. They named him William Willard, but we always called him Willard. A neighbor woman helped Letha with the work while Mother was in bed with the new baby.

A few days later as two neighbor men walked along the road past our house they noticed a blaze around the chimney on top of the house. They ran up and told Dad. They poured water into pails from a twenty gallon keg that we hauled water in, and soon put out the fire. We wanted Mom to take the baby and get out of the house, but she calmly told us she must stay in bed with him as it was too cold to take him out.

Someone from Omaha purchased the Wolf place, and so we moved into the house where Combs had lived on Lonergan Creek. Meanwhile, the Combs family had moved to a claim further up in the sandhills.

Seems like we were always crowded, and did not have much of this world's goods. Still, Mother always sang at her work. The first thing I would hear when I awoke in the morning was Mother humming as she got breakfast. She was such a fine seamstress. She not only made all of our dresses and underclothing, but Mom made leggings for us to wear in the winter snows. She made feather beds from the mountains of feathers off the ducks and geese Dad hunted. Once she even made a coat for Dad out of coyote fur from pelts that he trapped and tanned himself. Mother pieced quilts and coverlets from the scraps and remnants left from making our clothes.

Dad found that if he smothered a trapped skunk it wouldn't stink like skunks usually do. He then rendered the fat and got an oil that was useful for many things. Mom would sometimes braid a wick of cloth strips which she placed in a container of skunk oil to use as a lamp if we were out of kerosene or candles. I remember so well the sight of my mother reading to us by the light of the skunk oil lamp.

Dad didn't like to read himself, but he liked to listen to Mother read aloud. The few books they owned included a collection of sermons and essays. Dad particularly liked to listen to one by Stephen DeWitt Talmadge. Mother often read from her Bible to the family. On birthdays we played a game by making a wish and asking mother to open her Bible just any place. If the open pages included the words "...And it came to pass..." we took it to mean that the wish would come true.

One warm day that spring we all went swimming in a shallow lagoon that accumulated from melting snow after a thaw. None of us could really swim, so Dad put us on his back and swam with us. We were in the water quite a while and when we returned to the house, we began to scratch ourselves. All six of us were covered with chiggers. Mother really had her hands full with all of us scratching like gold diggers. Dad saddled his white Indian pony and rode twenty miles to Ogallala to find out what to do for us. Dr. Hollingsworth told him to rub us lightly with kerosene. Later we found that salty bacon grease is just as effective.

When I was eight years old we moved up into the hills to the Fish place, which was only a quarter section of land with a small one room sod house and sod barn. It was just a place to live while Dad farmed a little on two other places that had no buildings. We plowed up a small place for a garden. A dug well there barely supplied the house with water, so Dad sunk a barrel in a low place a quarter of a mile or so from the house where the horses could drink. When Dad came in from the other fields with a team, he would put two of us girls on the horses and send us down to the barrel to water them. In dry weather the water would be so low in the barrel that the horses would have to kneel down to drink. I would have to cling to the harness to keep from falling off. When it rained there would even be a little pond around the barrel. We girls often played there.

That house was so small that when we finished eating we would put the chairs outdoors so we would have room to get around. They set up two beds and made beds on the floor for us smaller children.

Towards fall when the wild fruit was ripening down on Lonergan Creek, Mom and Dad took the wagon and the older three children to the creek to pick fruit. Eva, Elsie and I stayed home. I was supposed to keep Old Nell, the work mare, out of a wheat field that belonged to a neighbor. We ran wild over the place all day, and I can't seem to remember what I got us to eat except for some raw lambsquarter greens that we picked. I put vinegar on the greens, but we didn't like them.

It was getting dark that evening when Elsie and I saw Old Nell going toward the wheat field. Eva was asleep in a trundle bed that pulled out from under the other bed. Elsie began to cry, so I put her to bed with Eva, and took a rope to go down barefoot across a prairie dog flat full of cactus. I caught the mare and led her back to the house. I slipped a picket rope around her neck and staked it out for the night. The dear Lord must have guided those feet of mine, for I did not step on any rattlesnakes or cactus, although both were frequent in that pasture. I went to bed and didn't know when the rest of the family returned.

Our closest neighbors that summer were the Schmidts. They lived in the same valley on a half section of land where they had planted cottonwood trees and some box elders. It was the only grove of trees for miles around in that whole country. We visited the Schmidts often that summer. They had three daughters about our ages.

That fall of 1895 we moved into Ogallala for the winter. It was the only time we children went part of a term of school in town. A Miss Carrie Robinson was our teacher, and we all liked her very much. The Combs family also moved into town that winter so we had some of our old schoolmates to break the the loneliness for us. Many moonlit nights that fall before winter set in the Combs children and a few of our new acquaintances would play Run, Sheep, Run with us in the open space near where we lived.

Mother joined a ladies' Bible study group that fall. I remember she went to a meeting one afternoon, and left Elsie to watch the baby (Willard) and also to tend a pot of beans simmering on the stove. Elsie forgot about the beans. The pot boiled dry, and soon smoke began to roll from the kitchen stove. Elsie grabbed the baby and the powder can and ran from the house. She was only six years old, but she already knew what came first in our household. Mother soon came home and set things to rights.

Dad still did a lot of hunting to provide the meat for the family. Sometimes he would be gone hunting for a week or more, and would bring back deer, antelope, prairie chickens, and grouse as well as quantities of ducks and geese. His men friends would often come and sit for hours listening to tales of hunting. One man who lived near us in Ogallala often came to swap yarns. One day Dad bought two hogs and hired that man to help him butcher. The town slaughter house near the railroad tracks belonged to Pete Girmann, who ran a store and meat market in Ogallala at that time. Pete gave Dad permission to use it. They finished the butchering just before supper time, and so they left the meat there to cool out before bringing it home. Although Dad invited his helper to supper, the fellow refused, saying he must get home to his family, so Dad gave him some liver as he left.

As usual someone was at our house for supper that evening, and they sat a while afterwards visiting and telling hunting stories. Later Dad recalled hearing a wagon rattle by while he sat talking. Later he and another neighbor drove down to get the meat with a team and wagon. One of the hog carcasses was gone. Dad was as sure as he could be that his helper of the afternoon took the meat, but there seemed no way to prove it. Subsequently he learned that this man was always getting into trouble. He spent so much time in jails around the country that he called them his offices.

We moved from Ogallala the next spring to a farm nine miles southeast of Ogallala. I was nine years old. We girls hoed the corn patch Dad planted there that summer as well as a patch of onions we planted along the South Platte River bottom. We lived in a small frame house near the August Hansmeier family, who were recent homesteaders from Germany.

It was a very dry year, and by midsummer, the corn turned brown and died. The onions flourished, however, because they could be watered by hand from the river. Dad couldn't find a way to market them though. The Union Pacific Railroad wouldn't ship less than a carload of produce. Most of the onions spoiled because we could only sell a few locally.

It was August, and Dad went out to hunt game for the family table. A few days later he returned full of plans for a new venture. He had learned of a hay contract to be let by the Ogallala Land and Cattle Company, a big ranch with headquarters in the North Platte River valley. Although it was owned by William Paxton of Omaha, the ranch was managed by James Ware and Bill Kosten, and it was these men with whom Dad contracted. He made a deal to cut, rake, and stack hay from the bridge north of Ogallala as far east as the west branch of the Birdwood Creek on the North Platte River Valley.

Others, including the Patrick and Mentor men, had tried this hay contract before and they had all lost money at it. Dad was certain he could succeed where they had failed. He began to locate more horses and some hay machinery. Letha and Edna were old enough to work in the field, and he hired some men to complete a crew. Mother prepared to go along, and to move once again. It was a tremendous undertaking for our family. Also an exciting adventure.

Author's notes

1) Grandma Berry told about her parents' meeting and courtship several times. When Great-Aunt Eva Samuelson died our cousin Laddie sorted through her many keepsakes and family memorabilia and actually found the letter mentioned in this account. Fortunately I phoned him when I first began to write these stories down, and he read it to me over the phone including much of the spelling that was so "original".

2) Great Grandma Stansbery's Bible was eventually given to me after the death of Uncle Willard, who had it among his things. That Bible was of infinite help in putting together this chronicle of a time two generations before my birth.

3) A timber claim was a quarter section of land that a settler could file on like a homestead, only the requirements for proving up after five years included the planting and cultivation of a specified number of trees. A relinquishment was a claim that someone had already filed upon, but had not improved and lived upon the complete five years before he wanted to leave. The claim could be sold to another settler to finish the improvements and the terms of the claim.

HAY CAMP AND THE CLAIM ON LONERGAN

Author's notes and asides:

The terrible winters on the High Plains during the Eighteen Eighties caused disastrous cattle losses. Speculative cattle investments by foreign and eastern United States entrepreneurs to stock the western open range had resulted in wide spread over-stocking and subsequent over-grazing of the vast range lands. With no provision for winter feed in case of deep snows, when the 1886 and 1887 blizzards ravaged the plains, cattle died of cold and starvation by the thousands. It was known in the cattle country as The Big Die-Up. The cattle bones from this catastrophe and the buffalo bones left from the wanton killing of buffalo herds that preceded the cattle were a source of income for the homesteaders who began to settle in Keith County in the late 'Eighties and early 'Nineties. Some gathered the bones by the wagon load to be shipped east on the railroads for making bone meal and fertilizers.

The terrible losses burst the speculative bubble that had become the western cattle business, and many of those who had called themselves "cattle kings" went broke and left the open ranges for good. Those who elected to stay had learned a hard lesson: To winter cattle on the high plains, winter feed must be provided. This meant putting up hay in the summer for use in the winter. Hay could best be cut on the river valleys and along creek banks and lake shores where these wetlands existed.

Bill Paxton, one of the most powerful and financially successful of the open range cattle kings, elected to stay, rebuild his herd, and provide winter feed. To accomplish this last goal he succeeded in gaining control of the North Platte River meadows for nearly 20 miles east and west of his Keystone ranch headquarters.

When W.P. Stansbery negotiated that first hay contract, Paxton's brother-in-law, James Ware, was his foreman and also a partner. Ware in turn had an overseer whom Edith Berry recalls in this chapter. The un-named overseer was known to have sought feminine companionship among married women, a most unhealthy practice on the frontier. After a late night on the town, he was found next morning face down in the sand at an unopened gate, with his saddle horse patiently standing nearby. The sheriff, whose wife may have been one of the aforementioned women, declared the cause of death to be heart failure, and dismissed the case. It was observed by some that a heart could generally be depended upon to fail if there was a bullet in it.

Edith Berry's Recollections continue.

"We began a whole new life that late summer of 1896. Dad planned for the whole family to go along to hay for Paxton. Mother was to cook for the crew as well as the family. We took along the milk cow and the laying hens as well as the cook stove, the kettles, dishes, feather beds, and other bedding—-all loaded on to wagons and a hay rack. Dad went into town to buy supplies at Axel Nelson's store.

He warned Nelson, "I won't be paid until the stacks of hay are measured." Nelson agreed to sell the supplies to Dad on credit and said that after the hay was measured would be plenty of time to pay.

Mom and Dad couldn't take all of their household furniture and belongings with them to the hay camp of course, so they left me there to sort of look after things. I was to stay with the August Hansmeier family who homesteaded near the house where we lived. Like many of the southern Keith County settlers the Hansmeiers were German immigrants.

I was to keep an eye on things and help the Hansmeier family by getting in the cows and gathering eggs and such work as a child of that age could do. They had two girls younger than me and a small baby. Although they were very kind to me, they often spoke German among themselves and I soon became so homesick for my own people I could hardly stand it. I was just nine years old.

I wrote my first letter to tell Mom I was sick. It was quite a while before she got it, and they assumed I was only homesick so they didn't come right away. Dad hired most of his crew from the neighboring families around the German neighborhood, and he eventually sent a young man back after a hay rake. The rake was equipped with shafts, and had to be pulled into the blacksmith shop to have the shafts replaced with a tongue so the rake could be pulled with a team of horses rather than a single horse.

When the man came for the rake, I begged to go back to hay camp with him, and at last he gave in. I rode the nine miles into Ogallala on the rake. After he left it at the blacksmith's I climbed up behind the saddle, and the two of us rode that very weary horse the fifteen miles to the North Platte River Valley and the hay camp. I was a tired, but happy, child when I crawled into bed with two of my sisters late that night.

My sister Ethel went back to stay with the Hansmeiers near our home. A couple of weeks later she wrote that she was sick. Dad was so busy, and he thought it was just homesickness again, so he did not go after her. On a Sunday shortly afterward a neighbor brought Ethel over in his buggy. She had some liver ailment that made her eyes and skin yellow with jaundice. Dad felt bad to think he hadn't gone after her right away. Ethel got well as soon as she was under our mother's care again, but she was never a rugged person, and did not work in the hay fields. She helped mother around camp and watched the younger children. After that none of us went back to the farm until haying was over in the middle of September.

Our camp had three large tents pitched near enough to the river for us to carry water to camp. There were stands of horse weeds that grew taller than a man's head along the river, and Dad would pitch the tents near these so they could serve as screens for a toilet area near each tent. The men he hired slept in one tent, the second tent was where Mom prepared and served meals, and the third one was where our family slept. Sometimes Dad drove a pipe into the sand and attached a pitcher pump with which we could pump water. Often the water from this shallow well tasted bad.

Fuel for the cook stove was always a problem, because there were scarcely any trees along the river valley yet. We picked up any fence posts that were broken off in the very few fences along the valley. For that matter Dad was not above sawing off a foot or so of a tall fence post for the cook stove. Mostly we burned cow "chips", the dried cakes of manure left by Paxton's cattle.

Mom had the cook stove placed under a makeshift tarp beside the tent where we ate so it wouldn't heat up the tent so much. She baked eighteen loaves of bread twice a week, as well as many pans of biscuits and corn bread. We girls helped peel ever so many potatoes each evening before we went to bed and set them in water for slicing into a hot skillet for our early morning breakfast. We took along a cow and the chickens to hay camp, so each morning while Mother fixed breakfast with us girls, Dad and the crew milked the cow, fed and harnessed the horses, and oiled the machinery. At six o'clock we served breakfast to a table of men, and then a table of our family. As soon as breakfast was finished Dad, Letha, Edna, and the men of the crew set out for the hayfield.

Mother and the younger children cleared the table, and while Eva and Elsie did up the dishes, Mom strained the fresh milk and set it in cans in either the river or a spring to cool. Then she began to prepare the noon meal. We kids would feed the chickens and sometimes we did the laundry by hand near the river and hung it on a make-shift line to dry. It was often very hot working in the tents and outside as well. Always there was water to carry from the river or the pitcher pump.

Flies were quite a nuisance. Sometimes in the evening Mom would kill the flies clustered under the dining tent poles by lighting a swatch of paper and brushing it quickly over them. Sudden thunder storms and gusts of wind occasionally caused the tents to collapse over sleeping children and others who had gone to bed.

We didn't usually hay on Sunday. One Sunday James Ware's partner and overseer rode by the hay camp when the men of the hay crew were playing baseball. He complained to Dad that they should be at work in the field, and that surely the hay was ready to rake or stack. Dad informed him that the crew needed rest, and that it was not his policy to work on Sunday. Although the ball players quickly volunteered to finish stacking the hay that was down the overseer was not popular with any of us after that. Funny thing about that man, he was found dead a few months later at an unopened gate. Some one besides the hay crew didn't like him I guess.

When the hay was finally measured, and the contract paid, Dad paid Axel Nelson and found he had a nice profit for the family to live on during the winter. Just for the winter we moved into the Combs house over in the old neighborhood on the North River. The Combs family had gone further north into the sandhills to take a homestead, so Dad rented the house on the river bottom that winter. It was quite comfortable and had a hard wood floor in the living room that all the neighbors used to like to dance on.

It was a happy time, and we were more comfortable than usual. Dad trapped along the North Platte and Lonergan that winter, and in the spring he filed a homestead claim of his own. After ten years in Keith County he knew it better than nearly anyone. He found that the land along Lonergan Creek was still public land and had not been filed upon for a homestead.

Most settlers preferred flat land suitable for farming, so they filed claims away from the breaks and sloughs of the twisting, winding course of Lonergan Creek. To Mom and Dad, though, the good water of the creek, the beauty of it, and the

13

prevalence of wild fruit and game along it seemed a paradise. Dad filed on a mile long narrow strip that took in nearly the entire length of the creek.

Dad began to collect materials to build a house on the claim. He sometimes bought existing buildings and put us girls to work tearing them down. There was an abandoned house on the North Table between the rivers that he tore down. The neighbors joked about the coyotes eating the house, as Dad tore it down and hauled it away on his wagon.

When mid-summer came, we prepared to go haying again. Dad contracted this year with young Bill Paxton, the son of cattleman William Paxton who was living with his bride at the Keystone ranch headquarters that summer.

Dad's crew the next few years included Will and Ed Draves, Bill Pankonin, August Behmer, Ed and Max Kurkowski, John Will Reed, Charles, Tom, and John Samuelson as well as our family. Later Dad hired the Coates brothers and their teams of horses as well.

Charles Samuelson worked most of the time as Dad's repair man and sickle sharpener. If it was necessary for him to work in the field, he always mowed. Letha and Edna worked in the field, and that second summer I drove the stacker team, even though I was only ten years old. After the first two seasons, we didn't stack the hay, but swept it into sweep bunches that Paxton's crew turned cattle on to during winter.

Letha always drove the lead mower. Dad said she was better at laying out a "land" than anyone else. He would ride his saddle horse off in the direction he wanted to cut, and Letha would mow towards him in a straight line. When she reached him, Dad would ride off at a right angle and she would repeat the process. In this way they laid out a rectangle, and then the other mowers would fall in behind Letha and mow until all of the hay in the "land" was cut.

I was pretty young, but I drove the stacker team most of the time. Just for a brief time I stayed back with a neighbor family to watch over our belongings at the Combs place. I knew these neighbors well and had gone to school with their children the fall before, so I didn't mind so much this time. However, I was glad when Mom and Dad decided to let me go haying, and sent Ethel to look after things at home. Elsie raked the scatterings that summer some of the time.

Dad oversaw the work and the horses. He kept track of everything, and he was always the one who decided when the hay was dry enough to rake, or stack, or bunch. He also hunted regularly to provide meat for Mother to cook. He often shot prairie chickens, and late in the summer he got curlews and occasionally venison.

We worked on through the summer and early fall, always going eastward, and leaving behind the shorn meadows and neat stacks or hay bunches for Paxton's hungry cows to eat during the winter. In October we arrived near the homesteads of the Brogans and McFaddens, Irish immigrants who had taken claims north of Paxton. Mike McFadden was stacking hay also and he jokingly remonstrated with Dad.

"Stannie, get on home with ye, so I can get my hay up. My men keep stopping to see which of those sweep bunches the sunbonnets is behind."

That was as far as Paxton's territory went, and we were soon finished. We went home for the winter to the Combs place again. On October 10, 1897, A neighbor woman helped deliver another Stansbery daughter. She was named Beatrice, but we always called her "Bea".

Dad finished building our house that winter and spring. We girls helped any way we could with it. Letha helped with the actual sawing, fitting, and nailing. Elsie and I worked with blocks of hair from the lumber yard that had to be separated for adding to the plaster when it was mixed. Dad double plastered the house for extra warmth. He plastered the outside wall between the studdings, then nailed lath on the studs in the usual fashion and plastered the inside walls.

Our new home had two large rooms, each sixteen feet square, one for a kitchen and dining room, and the other for a living room and parlor. There were two eight foot square bedrooms off the living room on the south, and two more eight foot square bedrooms off the kitchen on the east. There was an outside door into the living room on the east side of the house.

We moved in that spring. It was the first house Mother had lived in that she could truly call her own. It seemed to all of us a very special place. Dad planted an apple and cherry orchard right away, and we put in a garden. It was home as no other place had ever been.

LONERGAN

Shortly after we moved into the new house on Lonergan Creek that spring the Combs family decided to move away, so my folks bought the Combs' cattle. Mr. Combs fitted up two covered wagons and the family prepared to travel to Missouri. The night before they set out, they stayed with us. I was eleven years old, and May Combs was a year younger. She was my dearest friend. It was hard to say goodbye to friends and neighbors who had been as close to us as the Combs family. I got a letter from May about the 4th of July that summer saying that they had arrived at their destination all right. We continued to write to each other for the next 72 years until May died in 1972.

Meanwhile, Dad was just as busy as could be around our new home. He bought a barn in Perkins County, and we girls helped him tear it down, haul it home, and put it together again. I can remember Dad up on the roof of that shed using a shovel to rip off the shingles before we tore it down. He always tackled any job with such will and determination, and he was always alert to any job he could do to make a little more money for our family's living.

For example he once contracted with Keith County to repair the the wood bridge across the North Platte River on the road to Ogallala. Traffic had worn and loosened the boards badly, and so the county commissioners hired Dad to turn the boards over and re-fit them so that the wagon wheels would wear in a different place.

All along the North River folks lived in dread of a high north wind when the grass was dry. Smoke along the northern horizon always meant a prairie fire. Sometimes lightning or careless smokers and campers caused these, but more often the cause was sparks from the Chicago, Burlington, and Quincy Railroad engines as they traveled along the track through the sandhills to Hyannis and Alliance. The track was nearly fifty miles away, but in a high wind prairie fires burned unchecked from the railroad south to the North Platte River.

William Paxton was particularly concerned for his hay meadows on the river valley. H.B. Read proposed a plowed fireguard must north of the river valley to extend from Otter Creek to the west branch of the Birdwood Creek. Paxton finally agreed to finance this if Read would find someone to do the plowing. It wasn't long before Dad heard of it and asked Read for the job.

Early in June Dad, Letha, Edna, and I set out with six horses and two gang plows. Letha drove three horses hitched to one plow, while I rode the lead horse in order to see the ground just in front of us. Edna followed with another team and the second plow. Dad rode ahead on a saddle horse just like when he laid out the lands to hay. He and Letha went west in a straight line as surely as though they had a compass.

We began the fireguard south of Read's Busssard headquarters and plowed west to the head of Otter Creek by noon that first day. After we fed and rested the teams, we started east and arrived back at our starting point by evening. The next day we moved over twenty feet from our plowing of the day before and repeated the whole process. After three days we had a strip sixty feet wide across the grass land bordered with four furrows of plowed ground and intersected every twenty feet with four plowed furrows. When the grass was dry enough to burn, Dad very carefully burned off the grass between the plowed strips. This made a fire guard sixty foot wide to protect the hay land on the river valley.

After we completed the fireguard to Otter Creek we began to work eastward toward the Birdwood. This stretch was much longer. We camped out, and without Mother to cook and look after us, we found it tiresome and unpleasant. Sometimes a rain shower would come up and get us all wet. We finished it all at last, though, and got back home on Lonergan just in time for the Fourth of July. There was a big celebration planned in Ogallala, but Dad was so tired from the fireguard work that he paid us each a dollar to let him stay home and rest.

By the end of July it was time to get ready to go haying again. That year Paxton wanted the hay sweep-bunched rather than stacked. We had a pretty good run and got back to Lonergan in good shape. That fall Dad and Mother gathered us all up and took us to Ogallala to have a family picture taken. It was the first time any of us had ever been photographed.

In 1899 Mother was pregnant again, and this time the work and everything took a toll. When she took sick early, they sent for Doctor Hollingsworth. He came to our house on the creek, and things didn't go well. He eventually delivered twin boys, but they did not live. Willard was particularly sad because he would have liked to have brothers. Still, mostly we worried about Mom and did our best to make things easier for her.

She didn't go along when we left that summer to hay. Dad hired Mr. and Mrs. Earl Wilson to tend camp and cook in her stead. It wasn't the same without Mother, and I remember once that I came in from the field tired and hungry and said as much. Mrs. Wilson replied rather sharply, "I never claimed to be as smart as your mother."

When the Spanish American War broke out, several young men in Ogallala volunteered to go fight. One of them was Billy Patton. He had an idea that they should take along a mascot when they went to war, and he had heard that Stansberys had an eagle. They came to Lonergan to ask Dad to let them take our eagle to the war in Cuba.

Truth to tell, Mom was actually responsible for us having the eagle. When we were still living on the Combs place she looked out the kitchen window one morning and saw a huge eagle swoop down and seize a mother cat who had a litter of kittens in a nearby shed. Mom usually left the shooting up to Dad, but there was always a shotgun and a rifle standing in the corner of the kitchen, so she snatched the shotgun, ran outside, and fired in the direction of the eagle and the struggling cat. Both the cat and eagle were hit by flying shot, and the eagle dropped the cat and then fell to the ground. We doctored the cat's wounds, and it recovered and raised the kittens. Meanwhile, Dad captured the eagle, doctored it, and kept it caged in a pen. He fed it bits of meat he took from the carcasses of the animals he trapped for their pelts. Dad was more than willing to let the departing soldiers take it along for a mascot.

By this time Dad taught us girls to help him load shells in assembly line. He kept a can of powder, a bag of shot, and capped shell casings that he bought by the hundred. One of us would pour a measure of powder into the shell, another tamped a paper wad gently on top of the powder, another measured in the shot——large for geese, smaller for ducks, prairie chickens, quail, or rock rabbits——,and another placed a wad of paper over the shot. Dad himself crimped the edge of the shells and sealed them. He generally bought his rifle shells already loaded, but he did have a bullet mold, and if necessary he could fashion a bullet by melting lead shot in a dipper over the fire and pouring the molten metal into the mold.

When Letha was seventeen she got typhoid fever. She was sick quite a while during the school session, and she insisted on returning to school before Mother thought she should. The fever came back, and she had to return to bed again for three more weeks. Letha valued education, and often said she didn't want to be a "dunce".

In 1900 she was nineteen years old, and quite a beauty. She was tall with brown hair and blue eyes that often glinted with laughter and good humor. She was so capable. Both Mother and Dad relied on her in so many ways. She helped Dad at the forge, drove the lead mower in the hayfield, or anything else he wanted her to help with, and she helped Mom with cooking, sewing, nursing, gardening, and preserving.

Edna was seventeen that year, and she, too, was becoming quite pretty, although she was shorter and stouter than Letha. Edna was easy going and good natured and would do anything as long as it was outdoors. She hated housework and disliked "being cooped up" indoors. Dad called her his hired man.

Ethel was Edna's opposite. She was much frailer and had lots less stamina than Edna. She liked sewing and cooking, and was better at the housework than any of us. Her features were finely drawn, and she was rather fragile. Ethel sometimes longed for nicer clothes and more opportunity to be "refined", as she would put it. She didn't work in the field much, and often stayed back at our home to look after things while we were away at hay camp. A neighbor girl, Hattie Shepherd, sometimes stayed with her, and occasionally I would return home for a weekend with her.

About this time Dad didn't have any trouble recruiting hay hands. Mother was a good cook, and it was a chance to be near those girls. The work was hard, but they were accustomed to that. We all shared adventures and good times. And music.

Believe it or not, music was what made life not only bearable in those days, but enjoyable. Most families had a violin, an accordion, a guitar or a mouth harp that one or more of them could play in some fashion. Dad soon bought a cottage pump organ for our home on Lonergan, and all four of us older ones learned to play it a little. Even at hay camp there was always a violin or mouth harp to listen to in the evenings. We sang songs together, and many times the family and crew danced on the grass in front of the tents while Charlie Samuelson played the fiddle. We girls got to be very good dancers.

In Ogallala they held dances at the Searle Hall in those days. It was built in the late 1880's to serve as an "opera house", though it was really more of a community center. We danced quadrilles, waltzes, and round dances——most of them to a caller. At the Ogallala dances there was usually music by a fiddler, and sometimes he was seconded by someone playing chords on a guitar or the piano. That old time music still thrills me and sets my feet to keeping time. I think if I were dying and could hear one of those old hornpipes played in the same old way, I would last a little longer.

Dancing began at eight or nine o'clock in the evening. At midnight there would be supper or refreshments served from food that families brought with them. Dancing went on until daylight most times, because that is when people could see to drive their teams and wagons or buggies home again. The dances were well chaperoned in those days, because everyone from young people to grandparents attended.

At first Dad took Letha, Edna, and Ethel to the Ogallala dances. Once after a dance became sort of rowdy, he told the girls that they must all stay home for a while. Dad reasoned that if decent folk stayed away, it would soon be necessary for those sponsoring the dances to insist on better conduct. He was right, and soon good behavior was restored to the dances. Drunkeness was simply not tolerated.

It wasn't long before Letha, Edna, and Ethel were quite popular at the dances. They soon had a number of beaus who asked Dad to allow them to escort the girls to and from the dances. Mother often sewed into the night to make the girls new dresses to wear to a dance or masquerade. She would help them pin their hair up in special ways, and sometimes her own hair was falling about her face from loaning the pins to one of the girls at the last minute as she saw them off to a dance with Dad in the spring wagon.

We often had social events in our own home in those times. Dad always brought friends and acquaintances home to dinner, and we had other gatherings as well. Mother and Dad both believed strongly in being good neighbors, and would always share anything they had. Our home was always open to everyone around.

Mom planned a birthday party for Edna and me the spring of 1900. Both of us were born on April 12th, but Edna was four years older than me. I was going to be thirteen that spring, and Edna, seventeen. Spring was late, wet, and cold that year. During March our neighbors, the Holcombs, went back to his old home in Georgia for a visit. They asked Dad to look after their place while they were gone. It was three and a half miles for us to walk to school that spring from Lonergan. Since the Holcomb place was much closer to school, Mom and Dad decided to stay there while Holcombs were gone, so we would be close to school.

Mother made Edna and me new dresses of white India linen for the party, and she bought small pins of blue glass beads for us to wear down the front of our new dresses instead of buttons. Even though it stayed cold and wintry, we were both looking forward to our April birthdays and spring.

At the very last of March a blizzard struck. Holcombs' cattle drifted before the storm out an open gate, and Dad and John Fernstrom, who was working for him that spring, went out in the storm to find them. They took a rope and tied it around their waists so they wouldn't get separated, and then Dad's keen sense of direction kept them from getting lost in the storm, for you couldn't see a thing in the heavy snow and wind. We were all very worried, but at last they returned with the cattle, which they penned up carefully this time.

When the storm cleared, the whole North River Valley was covered with drifts of wet snow that clogged all of the roads and trails everywhere. Travel was almost impossible for several days until it warmed up, and then there was mud and water everywhere. About this time Holcombs sent word that they would be arriving in Ogallala on the train. Dad hitched up the team to the wagon, and set out to meet them.

When he returned, late the next evening, he not only had the Holcombs, but a new family from Georgia that Jack Holcomb had persuaded to come live in Nebraska. The newcomers were Gus and Mary Bell and their two young sons. One boy, Jim, was the same age as Willard, and they became fast friends.

The travelers were all tired and hungry after the long drive from town, so Mother fed them all, and then made beds out all over the floors for all of us kids to sleep on. There were three bedrooms, and the grown-ups divided them up and retired. That night we all woke up suddenly when the plaster on the ceilings of one bedroom and the living room fell onto the floor. When Dad and Mr. Holcomb inspected the attic they found that the blizzard had blown a drift of snow through a small crack beneath the shingles, and as the snow melted it soaked into the plaster and eventually caused it to fall.

By the time we got moved back in our own house, the thaw had made all of the roads in the territory impassable. The birthday party had to be canceled, and Edna and I were terribly disappointed.

Meanwhile, Bells moved into the Combs house, which was still vacant then, and they were soon acquainted with everyone along the river. They seemed to fit right into the neighborhood immediately. Gus Bell went to work for some of the ranchers who had cattle in the sandhills just north of the river.

That summer we went haying again towards the end of July. It was pretty noticeable that several young men were trying to win Letha's favor. Charlie Samuelson was ahead for awhile, but when we got back that fall, it was young Will Draves she danced with in the waltz contest at an Ogallala dance. All of us who watched were sure that Letha and Will would win. They danced so smoothly that it seemed a glass of water on Letha's head wouldn't have spilled as they circled the long hall. However, the prize was awarded to another couple, and while many protested and accused the judge of favoring friends, it really didn't matter. We all had a lot of fun, and enjoyed the music and getting together.

Soon afterwards Letha became engaged to Charlie Samuelson. He left for Oregon to earn money in the lumber industry with which he hoped to set up housekeeping. Soon after he was gone he sent Letha a ring of gold with an opal in the center surrounded by pearls. It was the prettiest ring I had ever seen. Later on Charlie came back, and by that time Letha decided that although they were fast friends, she didn't want to marry him. She returned the ring, but Charlie refused it, so she gave it to me——I always liked rings.

I sort of envied my older sisters a bit then. Although Dad and Mother occasionally allowed me to go along with them to dances , I was still too young to take part. And now that all of them had beaus, I felt very much left out. I received letters from May Combs regularly, and that spring I got one from her brother, Clark, asking me to marry him and come with him to the St. Louis Fair.

Well of course I wrote him I couldn't consider such a thing, but nevertheless, it made me feel good. My sisters teased me a lot by singing a new song that was going around that year. It began, "Meet Me In St. Louis, Louie, Meet me at the Fair..."

The Combs brothers, Clarence and Clark, came through on a visit in 1901. They happened to be staying with us in November when our youngest brother was born. Mother took sick while Dad was away, and she had one of us call Clarence Combs to go get a neighbor woman to come at once. By the time Dad returned, the neighbor lady had delivered a baby boy. He was born November 26, 1901. They named him Kenneth, and he was the youngest and last child in our family. Letha was twenty years old—-I was fourteen.

Clarence and Clark Combs soon returned to their family in Missouri and we never saw them again, for later the family moved to Montana. However, May and I always continued to write.

BELLES AND BEAUS

By 1902 the North river neighborhood around Lonergan Creek was home to a lot of settlers who had all been there for several years together. We were all friends, and had shared a lot of sorrows and good times. We young people had mostly attended school together, worked together, and attended the dances, picnics and other social gatherings with one another. We were a scattered population that included the Patricks, Holcombs, Richards, Smiths, Mentors, Samuelsons, and McGinleys and recently the Bells.

More and more Letha favored Ed Kurkowski as her steady beau. At dances he was her most frequent partner, and since he usually worked for Dad during haying, he had lots of opportunity to look out for her and do special things for her. That summer of 1902 Ed rigged an umbrella over Letha's mower to shade her from the sun's heat and glare in the field. Ed was born in Germany, and he came to this country with his family when he was about twelve years old. He could both read and write German well, and he soon became equally fluent in English. In some way the family lost part of their funds on the trip to America, and consequently Ed had known real hardship and hunger. He always worked hard, and he learned whatever he needed to know quickly.

There was a photographer going through the country that fall. Dad got him to come out where we were haying and take a picture of the whole haying crew. It was quite a task to get us all in, because Dad wanted the teams and machinery in the picture as well as the people. Although most of the hay was sweep-bunched by that time, we still had a hay stacker with us. The photographer finally had us raise him and his camera up on a make-shift platform he made on the stacker teeth. By this means he was able to get a view of the hay bunches and the long valley as well as the sweep teams and drivers, the hay rakes and teams, and the mowers. Dad posed on horseback on one side of the picture and Willard stood in front. It was quite a large picture, and turned out quite well. Dad and Mother took a lot of pride in it. Most of the family and crew were in it, but it was hard to recognize some of us because of the distance. The umbrella over the lead mower, though, made it easy to pick out Letha.

By this time Edna and Ethel also had boy friends, and there were two of these they seemed to favor. Edna most often danced with Charlie Richards, and Ethel with Ad Patrick. "Ad" was short for Alfred. Charlie, the youngest of a large and strung out family ten children, was full of mischief. I first saw him playing a mouth harp along a street in Ogallala when he was about ten years old before the family moved to the North River neighborhood. Charlie and Ad were best friends, and did they have fun!

Once Letha was invited to spend the night with her friend, Bea Smith, who had only recently married Sam Smith. The newlyweds lived in a small house in our neighborhood along the river. As was often done in those days, the Smiths made a bedroom for a guest by simply hanging a sheet across one end of the living room. Well, Letha had just gone behind the curtain to get ready for bed when they heard voices outside, and the sound of harness jingling. Bea said she would go to the door, so Letha stayed behind the curtain.

Very soon two young women came into the room amidst much laughter and talking. They were Lou Antrim and Gertrude McGinley. Gertrude's family lived on the North River, and Lou was teaching the McGinley school that year and staying with the McGinley family. A few minutes later their escorts came in, these proved to be Ad Patrick and Charlie Richards! They were all on the way home from an entertainment of some sort, and in very good spirits. Bea was sort of embarrassed, and she told them all that Sam was away for the night, so they soon left without knowing that Letha was behind the curtain.

Next day she returned home, and naturally she told Edna and Ethel about it. That evening Ad and Charlie came to call on Edna and Ethel. Dad was always quite strict about us going out together, or otherwise being chaperoned. On this particular evening Edna and Ethel met Ad and Charlie and insisted on immediately going for a buggy ride alone. Charlie and Ad were a trifle surprised, but readily agreed. They came back quite a while later, rather subdued. My sisters got out of the buggies and flounced into the house, and the young men drove away.

Dad was both disappointed and surprised that they didn't come in and visit in their usual fashion. He also scolded Edna and Ethel for going out alone. Ethel said they had a very personal matter to discuss that couldn't be handled in the Stansbery living room. Edna agreed, and that was that for the evening. However, it all soon blew over, and the two couples were going out again.

There was a big Halloween Masquerade Ball in Ogallala that fall. I was just fifteen, but Mom and Dad let me go with the older girls. I danced quite a bit with Earl Hollingsworth, and when everybody gathered to have a picture taken about midnight I sat with him. How I did love to dance, and if I do say so, I was very good at it. Several young men paid quite a bit of attention to me, and by the time I was eighteen I had five proposals of marriage.

Early in the spring of 1903 we girls decided to give a neighborhood dance and party in honor of Mother and Dad's wedding anniversary on March 21. We invited everyone for miles around, and we baked and cleaned for days preparing for the event. We particularly invited the Bell family, and as it turned out, Mrs. Bell was staying with us at the time anyway. She was expecting a baby, and Mother had agreed to take care of her delivery.

Gus Bell was working for one of the northern ranchers at the time, and he stayed during the week at H.B. Read's camp on the old Bussard place that was usually referred to as the Buzzard's Roost. There was a young Texan in the country about that time, who worked as a cowboy for several of those ranchers. His name was Arelias Berry, and being from the South, he missed his own people a lot sometimes. He soon became acquainted with the Bell family, who were also from the South, and he came to regard them almost as family. He often detoured from his long rides to visit with them, and the day of our celebration he stopped at the Buzzard's Roost in late afternoon to visit Gus and spend the night.

Gus was preparing to come to our house and he told his young friend, "There's six or seven of those Stansbery girls. You better come along and meet 'em." Berry cleaned up, and came along.

They arrived early and Gus introduced the cowboy all around, and we all played cards until the other guests arrived. My older sisters all thought him particularly handsome, but I don't remember thinking much about him. As soon as the others arrived, the fiddler tuned up, and we all began to dance.

It was quite a successful party, and everyone danced until it was light enough to drive home. As the party broke up and people began to leave, a light snow began to fall. Gus Bell and Arelias Berry left too, but by the time they reached the head of the creek, it was snowing so hard that they turned back. They returned to our house to wait until the snow let up a bit or quit. Letha was still up and she made breakfast for everyone. Meanwhile, I had gone up in the loft to sleep because all the rooms downstairs were full. I was sound asleep by this time, and Gus and the cowboy rode off again before I woke up.

Gus soon informed me of their conversation as they rode back to the Buzzard's Roost. Arelias Berry was thoughtful, and apparently he had noticed from watching everybody at the party that Letha, Edna, and Ethel had "steady" beaus, for he asked Gus, "Are there any of those girls that aren't spoken for?"

Gus told him, "Well, Edith isn't, but she isn't quite sixteen years old yet."

"Tell her she's got herself a beau," the young cowboy replied.

A few days later a baby girl was born to Mrs. Bell with Mother's capable help. They named it "Edith" after me.

THE HAPPY SUMMER

The summer of 1903 was the last one we were all home together. Letha was engaged to Ed Kurkowski by then, and they were making plans to marry in November. I was particularly conscious of how close we all were, and how happy a time it was. I suppose I was also aware that summer would soon be gone, and with it somehow a major chapter in the lives of our family.

There was the usual frantic pace of hard work on the creek that summer. We had a large garden, and Dad had built a cellar near the house to store the canned goods and the root vegetables during the winter. It was lined with limestone and was surprisingly dry and cool all times of the year. We had several cows to milk, and chickens to care for, and wild fruit on the creek to harvest before the birds got it. Lonergan never failed us. There were chokecherries in mid-summer as well as currants to be made into jam and jell. At summer's end there were the wild plums and wild grapes to pick and preserve. Soon we also had apples and cherries from the orchard Dad planted. One year Mom canned one hundred quarts of cherries that we girls picked and pitted.

We all went to the usual big Fourth of July celebration in Ogallala that summer. I longed for a new dress, so Mother took me into Forsythe's Store in early June to choose some material. I picked a pastel pink and white lawn print, and I remember it cost Mother a nickel a yard. She bought seven yards, and well before July Fourth she had stitched up quite a beautiful dress for me.

It was late summer when I went to Ogallala again. I was with Dad, and we were already haying on the river valley just north of Ogallala on the Richards place. As Dad was driving the team of horses along, I noticed a horseman quite a ways behind us riding to catch up with us. I pointed him out to Dad, and after a minute of studying the rider he said, "It must be Berry——he rides like an Indian."

It was, and he very shortly overtook us. He rode along side visiting casually with us for the rest of the way to Ogallala. As we were unloading and Dad was putting the team in the livery barn, the young cowboy asked me to accompany him to a dance that evening in Paxton. Dad finally agreed for me to go.

We took the train from Ogallala late that same afternoon and arrived in Paxton——it was only twenty miles away——in plenty of time for the dance. I was sixteen years old, and it was the first time I had ever been on a train.

The dancers that night took turns calling the quadrilles and rounds. At last they asked Arelias Berry to call. Very soon I overheard a girl complain, "Why doesn't he speak up? I can't hear him." I had already noticed how soft-spoken he was and how his southern drawl made most others sound loud and harsh. He was attentive and polite to me and quite a good dancer. I had a wonderful time.

About midnight we had to leave and catch the train back to Ogallala. I stayed with friends, and he went to the hotel. Next morning he came by and wanted to drive me out to where the family was camped.

Arelias had hired a team and buggy at the livery barn, and he had a boy along to ride his saddle horse as far as the river. We set off in the buggy and I felt pretty smug as we drove into camp. There was at least one man on the crew that I hoped was jealous.

When we said goodbye, Arelias sent the boy back to town with the hired team and buggy, and he rode away to his work in McPherson County. I little knew what a distance that was, nor that it would be several weeks before I would see him again. It was also a busy time for cowboys.

Charlie Samuelson and I had a lot of fun together that summer. We both liked to write poetry, and I would make up crazy verses as I mowed or raked hay and then tell them to Charlie in the evening. He would then either add to my verse or try to compose a funnier one. He surprised me once by making up some sentimental lines, and I began to realize that he hoped I'd be more than a friend one day. I thought it over and was flattered. Deep down, though, I knew I didn't care enough in that way. I didn't really want to be serious over anyone yet.

Bill Conners took me home from a dance one night and asked me if I knew the words to the song, "Poor Charlotte". I did. We girls sang together a lot, especially when we were at hay camp, and we knew the words and tune to any song that anybody was singing then. I sang the whole thing in the course of the ride home. It is about a girl who went on a sleigh ride in the midst of winter without her coat and froze to death. Bill seemed to be much entertained by it.

We were haying northeast of Paxton in the middle of September. Mother was terribly surprised one afternoon when Arelias Berry drove into camp with a horse and buggy that he had hired at the Paxton livery barn. When he asked for me Mom said I was mowing and directed him to where we were working.

Charlie Samuelson was mowing behind me that day. When Arelias drove up by me, Charlie called rather angrily "Get out of the way so we can go on." Well then Arelias insisted that I drive the buggy back to camp while he took my team and mower. I'm afraid I didn't really appreciate his gallantry. That rented team was the poorest pair of horses I'd ever sat behind and the buggy was not too good either. I was dusty and sweaty, and certainly not looking beautiful. We girls wore plain skirts and long sleeved shirts in the fields. Mother made long denim aprons for us to wear over our skirts, and we wore homemade sun bonnets on our heads to protect us from the sun.

At camp I dived into our tent to clean up and change my clothes while Arelias unhitched my team and put it away. I came out looking considerably better, but still feeling flustered. He told Mom we were going for a drive, and helped me into the buggy. We went east down the river valley, and Arelias explained that he was in the territory because his boss had sent him and a crew to Ogallala with a herd of cattle to ship to Omaha. After they got the cattle loaded out, he had a bit of time to himself, and he set out to find me.

As we drove along, he handed me a pair of soft leather gloves as a gift. I thought gloves a strange gift. Although I wore gloves in the field all of the time, they were far different ones than these. Mine were stiff leather that didn't absorb grease easily with gauntlet cuffs to protect my shirt sleeves. The ones Arelias brought me were not at all suitable for field work, and it did not occur to me at that time to wear gloves otherwise. I told him I didn't really feel I knew him well enough yet to accept a gift. He smiled, took back the gloves, and drove on. We talked of other things, and soon he took me back to camp and returned to Paxton.

Next morning Arelias rode north again, but on the way he stopped to visit Bells. He gave the gloves to Mrs. Bell, and she was delighted with them. When I saw her some time after we were back from haying, she explained to me that in the South no matter what a woman did, she wanted her hands to be soft and pretty as though she did not use them for manual labor. Mrs. Bell smiled and gently added that in the South a lady always wore gloves out of doors whether she was working or not. When the haying was finished that fall we began to prepare for Letha's wedding to Ed Kurkowski. Mother sewed a beautiful white gown for Letha, and was disappointed that there were no white shoes in Ogallala to go with the gown. In her usual resourceful way Mother then proceeded to cover Letha's dark leather shoes with material matching the dress. The wedding took place November 18, 1903, at our home on Lonergan. A German Lutheran minister performed the ceremony, for Ed's people were of that faith. The whole neighborhood came. After a dinner that we girls had worked for days helping to prepare, there was dancing.

Immediately after Letha and Ed's wedding Edna and Charlie Richards announced that they, too, wanted to get married. I was surprised to learn they wanted to get married in January of the coming year. That meant we had to turn around and start preparations all over again. It seemed to me we should have had a double wedding at Letha's and Ed's celebration and saved a lot of work. Mom and Dad felt differently, though, and they immediately went to Ogallala for Mother to buy material for Edna's dress. It was winter and nearing the end of the year. There was no white material to be had at any store in Ogallala, so Edna chose tan linen. It was rather coarse material, but Mother made it beautiful with a lot of matching lace and insertion.

Charlie and Edna said their vows on January 6, 1904, before an Episcopal clergyman who came to our home from North Platte. The Richards family were of English descent and belonged to the Episcopal church. Once more the whole North River neighborhood came to Lonergan for the wedding and a feast and dancing afterwards.

From time to time I received brief letters from Arelias Berry that winter. It was spring before I saw him again. I felt neglected, because the fellows who had courted my sisters lived in our neighborhood and came to see them nearly every week. Charlie Richards teased me a lot, and sometimes said that the Texan didn't really care, or he would come more often.

I was delighted one day that spring when Arelias showed up quite unexpectedly. He stayed the rest of the day and all night, but was bound he had to get back to his job the next day. We walked out in the orchard the next morning before he left. The apple trees were in full bloom, and the blossoms were like a fragrant cloud. I wanted him to stay and go to a picnic we were planning. I had baked a fortune cake for the occasion. It had little tokens baked into it, and your future was supposedly foretold by the token you found in your piece of cake when it was served. Arelias thought it sounded like fun, but said he had to get back to the round-up. We said goodbye sadly, and he mounted his horse and rode away toward the cattle country.

27

We all went to the picnic by team and wagon to a canyon up the river quite a ways west near Ash Hollow. We all spread out the picnic baskets of food and had great fun laughing and eating and cutting up. Finally we cut the fortune cake and each person searched for the charm that was supposed to be in each portion. Ad Patrick and Ethel were engaged, and he found a dime and exclaimed "Money! I'm going to be rich!". In my piece of cake I found a small heart of blue glass.

When we finished haying that September, we were home on Lonergan again, and Charlie Richards came by one evening to tell us he planned to go visit Ed and Letha. Ed had taken a job with Ed Meyer's outfit up in the ranch country and Letha was cooking for the men there also. Edna didn't plan to accompany Charlie because she was pregnant. Mom and Dad talked things over with Charlie, and at last they decided that I could go along and visit Letha. I was overjoyed because it had been so long since I'd seen her.

We set out the next morning in Charlie's team and buggy with messages and parcels from the family for Letha and Ed. We traveled most of the day through the sandhills, and saw scarcely another human being until we arrived late that afternoon at Meyer's headquarters. Letha and Ed were overjoyed to have us with them.

I was soon surprised to learn that Meyer's ranch had a telephone. The phone was rigged to connect the various cow camps and outposts on what was known as the Forest Reserve and the far flung ranch headquarters to Hyannis. According to Ed and Letha, Arelias Berry was working at that time for Joe Minor, and he was at a cow camp not too far away.

Eventually they persuaded me to call him on the phone that evening. I was pretty shy about the whole thing because the phone was in the big room where Meyer's hands were gathered to eat supper. Finally, though, I did put in a call with Letha's help. As it rang through I could hear someone calling Arelias to the phone amidst laughter and good natured joking. Apparently Minor's crew was gathered for supper also. After I told him who I was and where I was, I asked him what he was doing. He told me that he had been elected to cook that evening and that he had made a pie. They had just given it to the hounds, and the hounds wouldn't eat it. I found myself laughing in spite of the audience around me. Arelias was so glad I was nearby and said he would be over first thing tomorrow.

When he arrived next morning, Charlie's team was patiently standing hitched to the buggy in the yard while Charlie and Ed were doing some chores at the barn and corrals. Arelias left his saddle horse in the yard and quickly came to the house. He asked me to go for a buggy ride with him, and then he hurried me outside and into Charlie's buggy. Away we went across the prairie. It was a fine morning, and we visited and talked together as we never really had before. We came to a sod house setting in the middle of open country that served as a store and post office known as Lena. I stayed in the buggy, but Arelias went into the store and soon came out with a bag of candy that we ate on the way home.

Letha watched as Arelias rode away, and then she asked me if I had kissed him goodbye. I shook my head, and then she scolded me for being so hard hearted. I was quite astonished at my sister, and said I didn't think it fair to lead a man on if you hadn't made up your mind about him. I was beginning to find, however, that the Texas cowboy occupied my thoughts much of the time.

A COURTSHIP BECOMES STORMY

Ethel married Ad Patrick at our home there on the creek, February 1, 1905. She was a very good seamstress, and made her own wedding dress. It had so many tucks and ruffles that pressing it vexed her to tears. She and Mother went to a good deal of trouble over everything. Ethel wanted her invitations printed, so Dad and Mother took her to Ogallala to have them done at the newspaper office. They invited all the friends and relations in the neighborhood for a big meal and a dance afterwards. I stood up with Ethel, and Ad's brother, Ethan, was his best man.

With all of the older girls gone now, I was really busy at home. Dad and Mother both depended on me a lot. When it was time to go haying that year, I did some of everything, although Dad did hire more men. Once that summer I attended a dance with Ed and Letha, who had come home for a visit. It was about the only social occasion for me that summer.

It was a very busy year for Arelias Berry also. He came as often as he could, and he wrote me letters and post cards from remote parts of the cattle country. Still, we didn't get together very much, and I began to feel slighted. One postcard he sent me had a picture of him riding a bronc named Dynamite at a doings up by Hyannis. He was gathering cattle that summer for some outfit that was going into receivership. He didn't give me many details, and they weren't any people I'd ever heard of. That fall he went to work as Ed Meyer's foreman. He was in charge of all of Meyer's cowboys and hundreds of cattle. It was quite an opportunity for him, but it meant even less time for him to come see me.

Charlie Richards kept saying, "...If he really cared for you, he'd find a way to see you." Well one day I was particularly lonely and I wrote quite a hostile letter to Arelias about his long absences. It wasn't in any way affectionate, but I had no idea how it would seem to him. As a matter of fact the letter reached him about the time he had a serious falling out with Meyer. After he read my letter he made a decision to leave Nebraska and return to Texas.

The first I knew of this was from Gus Bell, who arrived one evening at our home. Bell was working for Perry Yeast up in McPherson County at that time, and he and Mary and the children had been living in a little two room sod house at one of Yeast's camps. Gus had decided to move the family back to the North River before winter set in. He drove the long way down to Mother and Dad's place to visit and locate a place to live. Also, I think he wanted to be sure I heard the news of Berry's impending departure for Texas.

That evening after supper we all sat around telling each other the news and catching up on all the family happenings since Bells had been in the sandhills. At last Gus said, "Berry is going back to Texas." He told about the falling out in Meyer's outfit, and then just before we all got ready to go to bed, he asked if I would return home with him next day to help Mary pack up to move. Mother and Dad were not at all anxious for me to go, and Dad particularly said I had better not, as we had a great deal to do at home.

I did not sleep well that night. For the first time I faced my true feelings about that cowboy. I found that he was not just one of my beaus—-he was my love. I was only eighteen, but that night I knew the time for decision had come and maybe gone. By morning I decided I must return with Gus Bell and somehow see Arelias at least once more before he left. I did not ask Dad if I might accompany Gus, I simply told him I was going. Neither he nor Mother raised any further objections.

I set out about mid-day with Gus. He had to see Andy Tuckson on some business, so we detoured into the Reserve where Andy's place was located. It was nearly sundown when we got there, so we spent the night with the Tuckson family. Next morning we traveled on and reached Yeast's camp about the middle of the afternoon. During that long drive Gus Bell told me a lot about his friend, Berry. Gus and most of the men of the territory referred to Arelias as "Berry" or "A.B." I was probably one of very few who ever called him Arelias. By our journey's end, I knew quite a bit more about the soft-spoken Texas cowboy, and one way or another, it helped.

OGALLALA, 1900

Arelias came to Ogallala from Texas in late August of 1900. He was just twenty years old, and when he stepped down from the caboose of a cattle train that day he was carrying his saddle sewn up in a gunny sack and the rest of his possessions in a carpet bag. He had a month's wages in his pocket, and he was responsible for the cattle in the cars. Those cattle wore the Four Six brand of Burke Burnett, and were to be delivered to H.B. Read. Arelias was tall and dark, and considered handsome by most everybody—-not just me. I didn't know him at this time of course, but he always looked older than his years to me. He grew up awfully young, and had been making his own way for several years by the time he arrived in Ogallala.

H.B. Read was an Ogallala business man who dabbled in many ventures, and traded a lot of cattle. He had purchased the Four Six steers several weeks before on a buying trip to Texas. At that time Read had requested Burke Burnett to send a reliable man along when they shipped the steers north. It was a long haul from West Texas to Ogallala by way of Denver. Read wanted someone with the animals to look after them. Berry was one of Burnett's most trusted cowhands, and he had voiced a desire to go to Montana, so Burnett put him in charge of Read's steers.

Because his mother died when he was only seven years old, Arelias really had no idea why his mother named him "Arelias". It was not a common name even in the South, so even as a child folks called him A.B. Every so often he would acquire a nickname of some kind for a while, but generally people reverted to his last name or his initials. I asked him once what B. stood for. He grinned in the mysterious way he had and replied, "Butler". If it did, it was the only reference he ever made to it, and he never signed his name that way. I sort of thought he might have just said that as a joke. But I wasn't really sure. Soon after he arrived in Nebraska he became friends with the Searle family, particularly the middle son, Charles. As a sort of gesture of friendship, the two men "loaned" each other their given names. Not many called Searle "A.B.", but soon the cowboys and others in the sandhills took to calling Arelias "Charlie". It was a nickname he came to prefer.

Arelias didn't really have much childhood or family life growing up. His mother was Mary McCracken Berry, and most of the relatives knew her as "Molly". She married John Karr Berry, and they had four children before she died. Roscoe was the oldest, and Arelias was second. They lost a third son in infancy. Stella was the only daughter, and she and Arelias were always close.

After his mother's death, Arelias lived for a time with his uncle, W.T. Berry, at Rosston, Texas. W.T. Berry's wife, Eliza, was also of the McCracken clan, being a first cousin of Molly's. John Karr Berry remarried when Arelias was about nine years old, but the boy continued to live most of the time with his uncle. Somehow he never quite accepted his stepmother, Emma South, and really by that time he had grown apart from his father.

He must have been a sturdy, independent child, for he seemed to have earned his own way nearly always. During the winter he chopped wood for his uncle and neighbors around Rosston. When spring came he soon rode out to find work in the cow camps around that territory.

He first met Burke Burnett when he was only nine years old. Burnett and his cowboys were attempting to corral a herd of cattle in the stockyards at Seymour, Texas, but several youngsters perched upon the fence were scaring the herd away from the gate. Arelias was passing by and saw what was happening, so he ran up and grabbed the other boys off the fence. He thrashed the ones who objected and soon chased them all away from the yards. Later, after the herd was corralled, Burnett searched out Arelias to thank him. Burnett noticed the boy had very little in the way of shoes, so he immediately took the youngster to a local boot maker, and ordered a pair of boots for him. It was the first pair of boots Arelias had ever owned, and he was immensely proud of them. He and Burnett became fast friends.

Burke Burnett was an early settler along the Brazos River there in West Texas. He was one of the early ranchers who trailed large herds of cattle north to market immediately after the close of the Civil War. Burnett was a bit different than many cattlemen of that time and place. He insisted on operating on his own or family capital. He was proud of the fact that a cow or steer wearing the Four Six brand (6666) never went up the trails mortgaged.

Burnett often took the Berry boy with him and he began to hire him for seasonal jobs in his cow camps or other tasks about his ranch headquarters. By this time he was running cattle on the Kiowa-Commanche lands in West Texas and Oklahoma. Burnett was one of the first Texans to negotiate with Quanah Parker to use that land. Arelias told me that Burnett could read a man's face at a glance, and made few mistakes in hiring men. His foreman and cowboys were a very loyal and able crew. Arelias spent as much time with Burnett's cowboys as his relatives permitted, which as he grew older was more and more.

Sometimes Burnett took the boy to ride with him, and on one hunting expedition Arelias saw a man try to kill Burnett. The Texas rancher had a lot of enemies, and as A.B. was riding a ways to one side he saw someone come into view and fire a shot at Burnett. That shot went wide of the mark, but Burnett's answering shot was on target and the man fell dead from his horse. There was a trial and the Berry boy's testimony of self-defense cleared Burnett of a murder charge.

Arelias attended school whenever he was with his aunt and uncle, but he always claimed that most of the skills and knowledge that helped him survive he learned in the cattle camps of West Texas, particularly those of the Four Six outfit. One spring he rode out from Rosston to find work and he wandered into a Mexican sheep camp. They needed a cook, and so A.B. hired on until the cattle round-ups would begin. He knew how to fry meat and bake biscuits in a dutch oven over a camp fire, and he soon learned to like the red chili powder the sheepherders carried in their pockets to season everything including the coffee. You know, he liked hot seasonings for the rest of his life, but he quit drinking coffee after an old cowboy saw him take a dose of soda after supper one evening and advised him, "Son, if you don't drink that coffee you won't need that soda."

He learned to speak a little Spanish from the Mexican sheepherders and also from other cowboys. Most people in western Texas and New Mexico territory knew some Spanish.

When Arelias was sixteen a local horse trader hired him to break a bunch of horses one winter. He had a livery barn and he agreed to pay Arelias five dollars a head for each horse he broke. One of those horses bucked into the fence and crashed through. Arelias kicked loose from the stirrups, but broke some ribs. Then after that he rode one of the horses outside the corral, and the owner didn't provide someone to ride along and haze. When Arelias opened the gate and rode the horse out of the corral, it began to run. Arelias couldn't stop him, but he stayed on the horse as it ran and ran and ran—-until it dropped over dead. It turned out that the horses were corn fed, and uncommonly hard to gentle, but nonetheless, Arelias broke them.

In the spring he went to work full time for Burke Burnett as a horse wrangler. In a short time he was in charge of the remuda. Burnett bought a herd of unbroke horses in Arizona Territory and sent two young cowboys to drive them home to Texas, a distance of about five hundred miles. A.B. was one of the two cowboys. He and his companion rode the horses, one by one, as they drove them clear across New Mexico, and by the time they reached the Four Six outfit, the whole herd were broke to ride.

In the years ahead A.B. learned to be quite skilled in the work of a cowboy. He roped, rode, and endured a lot of hardship of one sort or another. He learned to shoot, and as was the custom of the country, bought a six shooter and wore it in a holster strapped around his waist. He also carried a rifle strapped to his saddle on the long journeys he made. At least once Burnett sent him up to ride the drift fence on the lands leased from the Kiowa and Commanche tribes in Oklahoma and Texas. Late that summer he and a friend rode into a little town on the Kansas border. There was a county fair and some horse races going on, and the two cowboys offered to bet that A.B. could ride a bronc with a dime under each boot in the stirrups of his saddle, and not lose the coins. Well, all sorts of people wanted to take the bet, and the two cowboys obliged. The local people found the worst outlaw horse they knew of, and after they had it caught and saddled, while it was still blindfolded, A.B. climbed on. They placed the dimes under his boots, took the blindfold off, and turned the horse loose. A.B. rode it through all of its bucking and thrashing around. When the horse finally stopped, he was still on it, and the local gamblers found the dimes still in place. The two friends collected their bets and rode away much pleased with themselves.

One summer during harvest A.B. rode into Medicine Lodge, Kansas, to try his hand at harvesting wheat, or so he said. He had an uncle, Bud McCracken, who was the sheriff at Medicine Lodge. A.B. did not stay there long, as he found he did not like harvesting grain, so he rode back to the cattle country.

Once during round-up the cook quit, and the boss asked Arelias to cook. He said that one day during branding there were quite a bunch rode out from town to eat with the cowboys, and he cut and fried a whole hind quarter of beef in big dutch ovens over the camp fire. He made biscuits, too, and lots of good gravy after cooking that much beef.

There wasn't much wood in that range country, and as the chuck wagon went along, they picked up dried cow chips and threw them into a canvas fastened underneath the wagon. When they camped, they had some dry fuel. Even if it was raining when they quit, those chips under the wagon were dry and ready to burn.

Arelias told about going back to visit his aunt and uncle and other relatives, and as he left town to go back to where his outfit was camped across the Brazos River, he passed a church where they were having a meeting. He stopped, tied up his horse, and went in. The congregation was singing a hymn called "There's a Light At The River That I Can See". Later, as he rode on, it was dark by the time he reached the river. He said, "I sure wished there WAS a light that I could see." He had to kick his horse off into the stream and ride across to camp in the dark.

He used to talk about both the Brazos and the Cimarron Rivers. He rode all through that territory, and always it was dangerous work. They had to watch for banks on the far shore when they were shoving cattle into a river to cross it, because the cattle would always drift a little with the current, and sometimes if the water was pretty high and they had to swim, the cattle could drown if they came to a bank. The cowboys had to always pick a place the cattle could come ashore. They had riders along side too, but once in a while a rider would go under also.

I remember once Arelias was reading the book, "North of '36" (Emerson Hough). He came to the part about taking a herd across a river, and when the girl had to cross on horseback, two cowboys tied their ropes to her saddle to aid her across. Arelias quit the book right there. He said no cowboy would have ever tied his rope to another rider crossing a river, as it would have been the worst thing he could have done.

He was twenty years old in 1900, and had seen most of the Texas Panhandle and western Oklahoma. He had listened to the old cowboys tell tales of the long drives north to Ogallala and on into Montana. He thought maybe there was more of a chance for a young man to own land of his own up there, and he wanted to go see the country. Just about this time Burnett needed someone to send north with Read's cattle, so he sent Arelias.

When that train load of cattle rolled into town that summer, Ogallala's wild times were long over, and the town sort of considered itself progressive and respectable. Most of citizens had quit wearing guns, and lots of folks felt that saloons should not be allowed on Main Street. Main Street was no longer considered to be the street running along the south side of the railroad, but the one running north and south across the railroad track known as Spruce Street. Still, it was not much to look at. To A.B. Berry it could have been any village along the Brazos from Seymour to Gainsville.

When he climbed off that train, he intended to continue on to Montana as soon as Read took delivery of the cattle. However, Henry Read immediately liked what he saw of the young cowboy, and soon persuaded A.B. that he ought to stay and take a look at the Nebraska sandhills. Read even offered him a job at the Buzzard's Roost cow camp looking after the Four Six cattle. In the end Arelias agreed to stay awhile and put off his trip to Montana. Next day he rode out with Read and his men to drive the Texas cattle to their new range. They went north from the stockyards past the ragged fringe of Ogallala and a barren hillside known as "Boot Hill", an abandoned cemetery of former wild times. The graves included many a cowboy whose luck ran out in this town on the trail.

BUZZARD'S ROOST AND SANDHILL COW CAMPS

H.B. Read's sandhill headquarters came to be known as Buzzard's Roost from the name of people who originally took a homestead there. They were Mr. and Mrs. Samuel Bussard, who filed in 1895 on a homestead claim just north of the Keith County line in the unorganized territory of Arthur County that was still administered with McPherson County. The Bussards built a small sod house on the edge of a wet hay valley on their claim. Mrs. Bussard was permanently crippled in an accident when a team of horses ran away with the buggy in which she was riding, so Bussard was anxious to leave this remote place as soon as he proved up on the claim. Read bought it from him then, apparently with the aid of a relative, John Read, who co-signed the deed for the property. H.B. Read and his men then named their headquarters on the Bussard place "The Buzzard's Roost".

The Reads promptly mortgaged the property to buy cattle. Most of the surrounding sandhill area was open range at this time—much of it on a portion of the U.S. public domain that had been designated as U.S. Forest Reserve. It was grassland as far as the eye could see, but the U.S. Department of Agriculture hoped to someday plant a forest there. Read's property was a sort of gateway to the Forest Reserve where cattlemen soon had several camps sprinkled across the sandhills. These usually had a windmill and tanks for watering livestock, a few pens or corrals, and generally a small shack with basic provisions for sleeping and eating. During the summer the cowboys stayed at the camps to look after cattle, mend such fence as there was, and keep the windmills repaired and working.

Read housed his crew or anyone he had looking after his camp in the Bussard's little sod house. He built a newer sod house for himself and Mrs. Read to use, although most of the time they lived in Ogallala. When Read and his men arrived with the Four Six cattle at the Buzzard's Roost, Elmer Watkins and his wife of a few months greeted them. (He always called her "Mate".) Watkins was studying to become a veterinary, and Read let them live there while he read for his degree. The cowboys aways called him "Doc".

The nearest camp north of Read's was that of the Ogallala Land and Cattle Company where Charles Searle was often in charge. Beyond that camp were the camps of Joe Minor, Andy Tuckson, James McGinley, Harry Haythorn, Ed Meyer—and Perry Yeast. Arelias soon made the acquaintance of all the men who frequented the camps on the Reserve.

Yeast was quite a colorful character. Arelias worked for him several times in the days when he first came to the country, and liked him well enough I guess. Yeast was a likable man himself and one who treated his men well, but other ranchers in the territory didn't trust him. He was NOT known as an honest man. In fact, Yeast's escapades were a source of many tales told round the sandhills.

I remember Arelias telling one time about seeing Yeast and a stranger at the stockyards in Ogallala. Unlike most who traveled the sandhills, Yeast preferred to go by horse and buggy rather than horseback, and so the two were sitting in Yeast's buggy and counting the cattle being unloaded off the cars. They seemed to be involved in some sort of transaction over these cattle. Later Arelias learned that the stranger represented an eastern insurance firm with money to lend, and he had loaned Yeast quite a lot of money on the cattle. The trouble was that the cattle coming off the cars did not belong to Yeast, and indeed he had never seen them before.

In October of that first year in Nebraska A.B. went to help Joe Minor drive a herd of cattle from the Birdwood Creek back to Minor's ranch south of Hyannis. The day they started out with the cattle it began to snow. It was a cold snow and much earlier than usual for winter weather, and certainly much earlier than a Texan was used to. Arelias had no overshoes, and no clothing that was very warm. Still, he stayed with the cattle, and part of the time he walked beside his saddle horse to warm his cold feet a bit. By the time they got to the Buzzard's Roost, his feet were badly frostbitten. They bothered him for the rest of his life in cold weather.

Towards spring several of the cowboys staying at the Buzzard's Roost decided to head for Ogallala for supplies and a bit of diversion. It was March 28—-A.B.'s birthday—-and he was twenty one years old. Mrs. Read exclaimed "But Mr. Berry, I thought you were older than THAT."

Arelias replied, "I'm not so damned old."

It was 1901 and in August Read shipped the Four Six steers to Omaha. He put Arelias in charge of driving the herd to Ogallala again and getting the cattle loaded on the train for Omaha. The herd included a few old cows, and as they started down the hill into Ogallala just before they reached the stockyards, an old cow turned back. Arelias sent the rest of the men on with the herd and went after the bunch quitter.

By the time he had her headed back to the herd, she was mad and "on the prod", as he said. He chased her down the hill past a little house with a fenced yard on the west edge of town. There was a pile of hay in the yard. The cow jumped the fence and went for the hay pile. The old man who owned the house and yard ran out to chase her away. A.B. shouted that the cow was apt to chase him, just as she charged. Well the old fellow ran for the house and tripped and fell into the hay pile. The cow snorted and hooked some hay over him with her horns as she ran on over him. Then the old man got to his feet and ran to the house. The cow was again at his heels, and he reached the door just in time to slam it in her face. In a moment he opened the door a crack and pointed an old revolver—-Arelias said it must have come over on the Ark—-and fired a shot at the cow. He missed, and shot again several times without ever hitting her.

Meanwhile, Arelias got the gate open and drove the cow out towards the stockyards. As he went, he met Dr. Hollingsworth coming back from a call in a horse and buggy. He asked the doctor to go past the little house and make sure the old man was none the worse for his tangle with the angry cow. A.B. was in charge of the herd, and he felt responsible for the old man's troubles. The doctor found an angry and shaken old man, but one otherwise all right.

The herd was soon corralled, but the train was not in, and the cowboys were told it would be a while before it came. They all went to the barbershop for a shave and a hair cut and met up with Doc Arrowsmith, Wes Holloway, Ed McGinley and several others. It had been quite a while since they had all been together, so they were having a lot of fun visiting and laughing. Very soon a stranger came in for a hair cut. He was obviously an easterner and a newcomer. Arelias could tell that the stranger was uneasy and had heard nothing good about cowboys out west. It was dark by that time and Arelias stepped outside with Arrowsmith. A.B. knew Arrowsmith always carried a gun, and because he had left his back at camp, he borrowed Arrowsmith's. Then he fired it in the air several times and waited. Very shortly the easterner burst out of the barbershop, and they could hear the quick click-clack of his feet on the board walk as he ran toward the sheriff's office. The cowboys inside soon joined Arrowsmith and A.B. outside for a big laugh. Arrowsmith took his gun and went home. Arelias and the others headed for the yards.

The train was in by that time, and they were busy for a while getting the cattle loaded. About the time they finished Sheriff Harrington arrived at the yards, and after they were through loading he walked up to Arelias and said with a grin, "Son, you better give me that gun until morning."

Arelias replied, "That gun went to bed a long time ago, and it's been asleep quite a while now."

A WEDDING AT HIGH NOON

Arelias worked almost a year as Ed Meyer's foreman. Meyer was buying land and cattle wherever the opportunity arose in his part of the sandhills, and his ranch was rapidly becoming one of the largest in McPherson County. Arelias was in charge of several men and hundreds of cattle spread over thousands of acres of the sandhill country. By the time Meyer bought the VLC (Valley Land Cattle) land, he owned a lot of deeded land. Some was fenced, but much of it was not. He still ran cattle on open range and the Forest Reserve.

A.B. was constantly looking after Meyer's far flung interests, most often in the saddle. He was always one to take his responsibilities seriously. It was his dedication to his duties to Meyer that caused me to feel so neglected that year. I saw him so rarely, and received short letters and post cards from him only occasionally. My sisters' beaus had lived nearby and came to call nearly every weekend. And Charlie Richards was such a tease! It was his sly words about "...If Berry REALLY cared he'd come see you no matter what." ...that finally combined with my loneliness and feelings of neglect to cause me to write that fatal letter.

I little knew, of course, what was really happening so far away in the sandhill ranch country. There were several Texans working up there by this time. They were all friends by now, and stuck up for each other. At one time or another most of them worked for Yeast, and from time to time there was friction between the cowboys from Texas and those from elsewhere. Arelias was in the saloon at Hyannis one time when somebody made a remark about Texans. It wasn't a compliment I guess, and he climbed up on the bar with his spurs on and made two long marks with his spurs and said, "I'm a Texan—-I'm a Texan", but nobody cared to argue about it with him then.

Anyhow, at the round-up that fall Meyer got into an argument with Arelias and remarked to the effect that "... all Texans are cattle thieves." Arelias hit him right away, and they had quite a fight. Arelias knocked Meyer down and demanded his pay right then and there. As he prepared to leave camp, feelings were running pretty high, and he couldn't be sure he wouldn't be followed. He wasn't wearing his gun, so he asked Bert Burgess to loan him a rifle.

As Bert handed over the rifle he said, "Now, it's only got one shell."

Arelias replied, "One's enough."

It was right after this dust-up that my letter reached him. It was not the sort of thing to cheer a man up. He decided to go back to Texas at once, and that was when Gus Bell set out for Lonergan.

We arrived that afternoon at Perry Yeast's eastern camp where Mary and Gus and their children were living in a two room sod house. Mary had supper early that evening because we hadn't eaten since we left Tucksons'. Just as we finished eating, Gus saw a rider come into the corral. It was Arelias with a stray steer of Yeast's that escaped during the fall round-up. Gus went right out to see him, and when Arelias heard I was there he prepared to ride on, saying "I don't think she wants to see ME."

Gus convinced him that indeed I did want to see him, and told him to come in and eat. Arelias had spent the whole day hunting that steer, and he hadn't eaten since morning. Meanwhile, Mary Bell scurried around and put a fresh batch of biscuits in the oven to bake while she set out the rest of the food from supper. Presently the men came in the house, and while he was eating Arelias tried to talk and joke in his usual fashion, but somehow the two of us found it hard to visit in the old way.

After he was through eating he asked me to go for a walk. It was just getting dusk, and we walked away from the house and corral up a hill nearby. In the end I let him know I cared a lot, and after that things were much better. From the top of the hill we could see a team and wagon going towards Hyannis, and with his arms around me, Arelias told me the wagon had his trunk on board headed for the Hyannis depot and the first leg of the journey back to Texas.

When he rode into town to retrieve that trunk, he was full of plans for the future and they didn't include Texas. We were not formally engaged then, but I guess you'd say we had an "understanding".

Arelias decided to work for Yeast that winter with Bert Burgess, who was Yeast's foreman. Arelias introduced Burgess to me saying, "I want you to meet a man who was run out of Texas for the same things I was." Both men worked for Harry Haythorn, who was Yeast's second in command in those days. Yeast lived with his family in Hyannis, and they were often away. (So many of those people lived in Omaha part of the time.)

I helped Mary Bell pack up their things to move back to the North River. They moved into the old Combs house for the winter, and it was like old times to have them nearby again. I was happier than I'd been for a long time, but also much busier. Mom was gone quite a bit down to Edna's. Edna and Charlie had a baby girl, Bertha, who was born in January of 1905, and now Edna was expecting another baby. Bertha was Mom and Dad's first grandchild, and they were much taken with her. They always loved children so much.

I did not see Arelias again until nearly Christmas. He came to Lonergan one day with a team and a new buggy he'd just bought in town. He and I drove to Ogallala. We saw Ethel and Ad, who were living in town that winter, and Arelias showed off his new rig and took them for a ride. Then Ad took Ethel by the hand and said with a mischievous twinkle in his blue eyes, "You two must have things to talk about. We'll be getting along."

Arelias drove east of town down a road along the South Platte Valley through King Feltz's place. He was quiet for a while, and then he asked me to marry him. I looked into those dark eyes and couldn't have said no if I'd wanted to. When I said "Yes", he immediately smiled and asked, "When?"

I guess I was a sort of at a loss to answer just like that, and finally replied, "March 21", which was Mom and Dad's wedding anniversary. His brown eyes looked wistful again, and then he said, "You wouldn't make me keep on batching just for THAT would you?" In the end I agreed to set the date a month earlier on February 21 of the coming year, 1906.

We went to a big doings at the Congregational Church in Ogallala that night. Nearly everyone in the whole country, including Mom and Dad and all of the kids still at home, also attended. Arelias stayed on for Christmas, and gave me a pair of ivory combs set with turquoise and five dollars as a Christmas gift. It was the most money I had ever possessed in my whole life.

He left Christmas afternoon, and returned to Yeast's camp in McPherson County. Ten days later I came down with red measles, as did Elsie, Eva, Willard, Bea, and Kenneth. In fact, everyone who had attended that Congregational Christmas party and hadn't had measles before, came down with them. We were all terribly sick, and Mother and Dad, were soon worn out trying to care for all of us at once. Charlie Richards came to visit, and after he saw how things were, he went to town and sent a telegram to Hyannis addressed to A.B. Berry. It simply said, "COME AT ONCE TO LONERGAN". He did NOT sign it.

Someone from Hyannis delivered this message next day to Arelias as he and another cowboy rode among Yeast's cows. Arelias read the telegram and turned to the other cowboy saying, "Look after everything 'til I get back." Without another word he turned his horse south and rode hard for Lonergan. When he arrived late that afternoon, he strode into our house out of the crisp, cold January air to find me and the rest of the family mighty sick, and both Mother and Dad exhausted.

Now Arelias prided himself on being equal to any occasion, and he took off his hat and coat and went to work. Mom found him to be quite a passable cook. A day or so later Cy Kelly stopped by to find Arelias frying quantities of pancakes. Kelly went on to Ogallala, and while having a beer at Manse Sheffield's saloon, he related the news of the measles epidemic on the North River. He mentioned seeing Berry at Lonergan cooking pancakes for the Stansbery tribe. Charlie Richards was present in the saloon——Manse Sheffield was his brother-in-law——and he began to laugh. When Cy Kelly told me about that afterwards, I immediately knew who sent the telegram.

When the worst was over, Arelias returned to the sandhills, and he soon left on a trip with Joe Minor to buy cows in Wyoming. He came back with 50 head of his own cattle from the PT Bar outfit.

By that time Mother was down to Edna and Charlie's again to help with another baby. It was another little girl, and they named her Letha. I went down to see Mom and Edna one day and finally told her I wanted to get married February 21. (That date was now only three weeks away.) Mom exclaimed, "I thought I told you to give me more time than the others did. This is less." And then she looked at Elsie, and said, "This has got to stop." We all laughed, for we knew she was referring to the fact that there had been a wedding every year now for four years, and Elsie was now only 16, and the next in line. It was Elsie I asked to stand up with me. I asked her if she would mind standing up with John Davis, whom Arelias had asked to be best man. Elsie replied, "Why, I'd even stand up with Roy S." (Roy was a boy who worked one summer in the hayfield and turned Dad in to the sheriff for shooting prairie chickens out of season. Needless to say, none of us liked him very much.)

I used my Christmas money to order several yards of white china silk, some artificial pearl orange blossoms, a hat form, and some lace trimming. I wanted a flounced slip, and began to make it while Mother was still at Edna's. I found sewing the lace between the ruffles very difficult. When Mother returned home, she showed me how to sew the insertion on the material BEFORE cutting the flounce. After doing this it was quite simple to cut the material between the two rows of stitching underneath the lace. Then she turned the material to each side. Mother made my wedding dress.

I wrote the wedding invitations myself in black ink on cream colored stock. These read:

Mr. and Mrs. Wm. P. Stansbery
request your presence
at the marriage of their
daughter,
Edith Ivy Stansbery
to
Arelias B. Berry
Wednesday, February 21, 1906
at high noon

The time passed very swiftly. Before I could realize it February 21 dawned clear and beautiful during a particularly warm break from winter. Everything was nearly ready for the festivities. I frosted two bride's cakes that morning while Mom finished preparing the rest of the food. Dad took Elsie and Eva down to the soddy on the river meadow to bring back extra tables and chairs. Late in the morning people began to arrive, among them Reverend Link, who was to perform the wedding ceremony. Most of the family were on hand by this time, and Ethel teased me as I went into the bedroom to put on my wedding dress.

"Don't faint if the groom is three minutes late."

Arelias was not late. He left Yeast's camp early that morning, and drove his team at such a rate that John Davis, who rode with him, expected to turn over at every turn. They arrived safely though, right at noon.

Everyone gathered in the living room then, and Arelias and I stood before the minister. Arelias looked particularly handsome in his black suit with a small black tie at the collar of his best shirt. I wore the white gown that Mother had sewed so beautifully and the girls had helped me sweep my hair on top of my head with the ivory combs in it. We exchanged our vows, and in a few brief moments Arelias placed a gold ring on my finger. Reverend Link pronounced us man and wife, and there was much hugging, kissing and well-wishing all around.

All of the married guests and the elder neighbors sat down at the tables in the big kitchen to eat dinner. The younger ones filled their plates and went out doors to eat at the chairs and tables set up there. After everyone finished the minister prepared to leave, and he told us with a smile to get on with the dance. Just as soon as someone could tune a fiddle, that is what we did.

About midnight Mom set out refreshments again, and then they struck up the tune "Jubilo" for Arelias, because it was a southern tune. When it started to get light our guests began to leave, and the family gathered around the pump organ and sang "God Be With You 'Til We Meet Again".

We all slept for a little while on beds and pallets strung around the rooms in haphazard fashion, and at noon we went down to Gus and Mary Bell's home for dinner. Arelias joked and laughed with Bells in the happiest fashion, and Mary Bell confided to me that I must bake lots of biscuits to keep a Texan happy.

That evening we all went to Ogallala for the Washington's Birthday Ball at the Searle Opera House. We danced until nearly midnight. During the intermission then Mrs. Harry Haythorn invited us all to her home in Ogallala for a supper in honor of Arelias and me. Afterwards everyone set out to return to the dance hall. It was then that Arelias took my arm, and we fell behind the others. When we got to the street corner where they turned to go to the hall, we walked on a different direction to the hotel where we could be alone at last.

A COW CAMP BRIDE

We returned to Lonergan next day and gathered up our wedding presents and my things. It soon was plain we had too much stuff to carry in the buggy, so Dad loaned us the spring wagon. Early Sunday morning we set out for Yeast's camp in the spring wagon loaded with dishes, quilts, a feather bed, and quite a few other things. We traveled much slower than Arelias was able to do on our wedding day, and it was late afternoon when we went around a fenced pasture in open country. Beyond the fence I could see a horseman who waved and seemed to be hailing us. Funny thing—-Arelias did not return his wave or seem to even see him. Normally he saw everything, but this time I finally pointed out the distant horseman, and Arelias just smiled and caused the horses to go faster.

We soon arrived at the two room soddy where the Bells had lived when I returned with Gus in the fall. It was to be our first home, and we unloaded our things from the wagon just as daylight was fading.

I was anxious to return Mom and Dad's wagon, but Arelias was busy all the time it seemed. He fed about 700 head of Yeast's each day, and it meant pitching hay on to a rack, and then forking it off along the feed ground. Sometimes he rode out to chase away the cattle that weren't Yeast's, because the range was mostly unfenced yet. The other cattle he chased away were usually Meyer's.

Two weeks passed, and there was a time of mild weather, so I decided to take the wagon myself. I left early one morning and very soon arrived at the fenced pasture Arelias and I had gone around. I now knew it belonged to Harry Haythorn, and the cowboy we had seen in the distance was Charlie McLaughlin. There was a gate across the trail and I decided to go through it because it would be so much shorter. I opened it, drove through, and closed it again with no trouble. However, further on there was another gate to get out of the pasture, and when I opened this one I drove the team through, and while I was closing it they headed on down the trail with the wagon. I ran to catch them but they were already beyond my reach. Just then I heard someone holler and looked back to see Charlie McLaughlin riding toward me at a gallop. I ran back and pulled the gate aside once more just as he raced through to overtake the team. He soon came back leading them, and was I thankful!

He told me when I returned to drive around because it was easier. I believed him. I drove the rest of the way without any problems and arrived at home on the creek that evening. The trip back with the buggy was uneventful, and I went around the fences.

Distance in the sandhills was something the people who lived there just didn't pay much attention to. I learned about it the hard way. Arelias asked me to ride over to Kaycee and pick up our mail one day that spring, and I quickly agreed to do it. I set off that morning riding his saddle on a gentle horse named "Red". I rode a long ways before I came to buildings or anything. In fact, they told me at the post office I had come about twelve miles. I got the mail and rode the twelve miles back to Yeast's camp. The next day I was so stiff and sore I could hardly move.

Arelias rented Haythorn's fenced pasture in the spring to summer his PT Bar cows. Before he turned the cows into the pasture he wanted to brand them with his own brand, which he called the Flying X. Charlie McLaughlin agreed to help him, and they had me open and close the chute gate in the corral. It worked by a rope threaded through a pulley overhead. Everything went along smoothly until they ran the last cow into the chute. I pulled the rope to open the chute gate, and the rope broke. I fell over backwards, and somehow the cow got away. Arelias and McLaughlin laughed and said I'd have to brand this one. They roped the cow and tied it up, and then Arelias carefully instructed me in the way to apply a hot branding iron. I did it and they said I was a real hand. I didn't much like the job, though, and to tell the truth, I was always glad after that to be too busy cooking to help at branding.

Charlie McLaughlin soon decided to leave the sandhills. He arrived at our house to say goodbye one day. He and Arelias exchanged spurs as a sort of remembrance, and I was a little disgusted because a day or so beforehand I had polished the silver inlays in Arelias's spurs until they sparkled and shone. McLaughlin's spurs were fashioned from steel mowing machine sickle sections. They weren't fancy in any way, but they were tough and indestructible, and they made a sound like no others. When I heard a rider coming I always knew if it was Arelias by the sound of those spurs.

The folks at home wrote me regularly. Elsie wrote once that Dad bought some Longhorn steers. He dehorned them and turned them down the creek. He left then, and Elsie went out to milk and found one steer bleeding badly. She ran to the house and told Mom, who immediately rushed outside and built a small fire to heat an iron rod. Mother took the red hot rod and seared the arteries on the head of the bleeding steer, and it lived. As I read the letter, I marveled once again about Mother.

I often rode with Arelias that year, especially on Sunday. We would go coyote hunting with a pair of hounds named Jim and Jody from the camp. They were good dogs, and we caught several coyotes with them. The thing was that we only had one saddle, and only two horses gentle enough for me to ride. I rode the saddle on Red, and Arelias rode the other gentle horse bareback. That winter there was a $2.50 bounty for coyote scalps.

We rode by the Haythorn pasture one Sunday to check on our own cattle, and found that the windmill wasn't pumping any water. The well needed new leathers. We had the leathers, but putting them on meant pulling the well rod. The only tools we had were a pipe wrench, a hammer and a screwdriver, but somehow we got it done.

We went down to Daugherty Camp for a while to help Bert Burgess deal with a new bunch of cattle Perry Yeast had bought. Those cattle had so many different brands that Arelias and Bert finally decided to just saw one horn off of each to identify them as Yeast's. Bert batched there in a sod house, because his wife, Belle, and their small son lived in Hyannis. (Belle was a Guilfoyle girl, and used to living in town.) I went along with Arelias and cooked for him and Bert and any other cowboys that came along.

Perry Yeast's son, Frank, often came to camp and sometimes stayed several days with us. He left his horses there, because he trusted Arelias with them. It was all right for Arelias to ride those horses, but Frank didn't want anyone else to handle them.

That summer there was a big doings in Hyannis, and Arelias and I were invited to stay at Yeasts' home. Mrs. Yeast was trying to get Frank up one morning while we were there, and she said to me, "Mrs. Berry, how do you get Frank up in the morning at camp? He's such a sleepyhead at home."

I laughed and said, "He sleeps in the kitchen, and he has to get up before I can cook breakfast."

It was in August that I looked out of the window at Daugherty Camp and saw a team and buggy coming down the trail towards the house. It was Ethel and Ad. Was I glad to see them! We had so much visiting to catch up on about the family and the North River neighborhood. Letha and Ed were at Chadron now where Ed was working for Casper Girman in a meat market there. (Casper had married Ed's sister.) Ethel planned to board the train at Hyannis and go to Chadron. Arelias thought it would be good for me to go with her and visit Letha and Ed too. He said by the time I returned he would be working for Joe Minor, and he would move our things to Minor's ranch while I was gone.

Ethel and I soon left on the train for Chadron, while Ad returned home. Arelias and Bert finished up at Daugherty Camp. When I returned, Arelias took me to Joe Minor's ranch headquarters. We were to live in the ranch house that fall and winter because Mrs. Minor was in Omaha putting their children in school. I was to cook for Minor and his crew as well as Arelias.

About this time it was clear we needed some furniture and dishes as well as a few other things. We ordered a bed and the other things at a store in Hyannis. Several days later our stuff came into Hyannis on the railroad, and the storekeeper sent a man with a team and wagon to haul the freight out to Minor's headquarters. He arrived about three o'clock one afternoon, and after he unloaded our things, he headed back to Hyannis. When Arelias returned that evening from work he asked me if I fed the man who had hauled the freight. I replied in surprise, "No, it was the middle of the afternoon when he was here."

Arelias reproached me, "There wasn't any way that man could have eaten his dinner anywhere else. He was on the trail all day with our provisions and furniture." (Minor's headquarters WERE quite a ways from Hyannis.) So after that I fed anyone and everyone who showed up there, no matter when or what.

After the round-up was over that fall, Arelias and I rode out with the hounds again to hunt coyotes. We had another saddle by this time, and we rode out together properly mounted. We did pretty well, and one morning in good weather we headed for Tryon, the county seat of McPherson County, to collect the bounty for our coyotes scalps. By evening we arrived at Yeast's Farm Valley headquarters where Harry Haythorn and his wife and two sons lived. Mrs. Haythorn's mother, whom everyone knew as Grandma Dunn, did the cooking for the outfit, and that very morning she had fallen and injured her right hand.

When we arrived that evening she asked me if I'd make the biscuits for her. Let me tell you, I had a few misgivings because she was known as a good cook everywhere around. However, I made the biscuits and everybody said at supper they were good. I stayed on at Farm Valley the next day while Arelias continued on to

Tryon by himself. I wasn't feeling well, and he could go much faster alone. When he returned I was able to ride back to Minor's ranch.

One day at noon as all of the hands were eating dinner, one cowboy mentioned that they should remove the shoes on Blue Devil, a particularly difficult and untrustworthy saddle horse. The group at the table that day agreed that there weren't enough men on the ranch—maybe not in Hyannis—to get the shoes off Blue Devil. They put it off for the present and left to see about other chores. I noticed that all during this talk Arelias didn't say anything.

After they left, I did up the dishes and happened to look out of the window towards the barn. Blue Devil was in the corral because I could just see his head around the corner of the barn. I thought I knew what was happening, but I went outside just to make sure. I crept around the barn and looked into the corral, and sure enough, there was Arelias. He had the horse standing in the corner of the corral with one hind leg tied up, while he calmly removed the shoes. It didn't do to tell that man that a thing couldn't be done.

Joe Minor often came in to ask if I could have dinner ready early because he wanted to send the men to some distant windmill or camp. I always said yes. Sometimes the meat would have been more tender if it had cooked a while longer, but somehow I would manage to get things on the table when he needed it.

Minor was building a feed lot near Hyannis that winter. It cost him quite a lot and strained his finances to the limit. Arelias told him that we would not draw our wages until spring except for what few things we needed to buy. By this time Arelias had it in mind to file a homestead claim and start a ranch of his own.

He rode to North Platte consult the United States land office there about land available to file homestead claims upon. The Kincaid Act had passed in 1904, and it was now possible to file on a full section of sandhill land. Arelias was familiar with most of the sandhill country north of the North River, especially that in the Reserve, and he had learned in Texas how to read a land description and decipher it.

I think it was in returning from this trip that he met up with an Indian. By this time the Indians were living peacefully on the Pine Ridge and Rosebud Reservations. However that evening as Arelias rode through the sandhills on his way back to Minor's ranch it was getting dark, and he saw a campfire in the distance. He approached it slowly and hallooed in the custom of the open range. A man welcomed him to share the camp, and when Arelias rode closer he recognized an Indian. They shared their supper and the camp that night, and the next day went their separate ways. Of course Arelias had known a lot of Indians in the days he rode for Burk Burnett.

The land Arelias chose to file on was a half section in Keith County just north of Mom and Dad's home on Lonergan. I was quite pleased to think of being close to my family once more. A Mrs. Kingsley, who was a recent widow, owned the other half of the section that Arelias filed upon. After her husband died, she wanted to leave the sandhills, so Arelias was able to buy her claim. It had a decaying sod house on it with a frame lean-to attached. Arelias bought it all as well as a few belongings—a cook stove, a cupboard, and a table— in the house that she didn't want to move.

In order to prove up on his own claim, however, he had to build a house there. He planned to do that during the summer, and H.B. Read told him that we might live at the old Buzzard's Roost quarters until our sod house on the claim was completed. After the spring work at Joe Minor's ranch was over, we moved to the Buzzard's Roost. I was pregnant by then, and the baby was due to be born in August.

I coaxed Arelias to plow a garden patch for me. He borrowed a plow and hitched our two saddle horses to it. These did NOT think much of the whole idea, but one way and another Arelias got it plowed—-sort of. I planted quite a few vegetables and took care of them that summer.

Elsie came up to be with me, because Arelias had to be gone a lot. Not only was he working on the claim and one thing and another, he rode up on the reserve and looked after cattle for Minor and some of the others who had cattle there. Elsie and I found a barrel of things stored in a shed, and it had quite a few comic papers in it. We had not seen any of these before, and we had a lot of fun reading them, especially one called, "—-AND HER NAME WAS MAUD", about the antics of a mule that got in and out of a lot of trouble.

Arelias and Charlie Searle came back from the Reserve one day and looked over the stuff in that barrel and found several sticks of dynamite. They took them away from the buildings and set them off like school boys on the Fourth of July.

I went down to the garden about the first of August and discovered a rattlesnake seeking the shade under my plants. I killed it. There were a lot of rattlesnakes along the North River when I was growing up, and I learned to kill them no matter what. I hated them, but didn't feel the way some people do. I didn't want one to get away.

About the middle of August Arelias took me to town to stay with Mrs. Manse Sheffield until the baby was born. Arelias rode into town most evenings to be with me. He was there the evening my pains started. That same night a party arrived in town with a boy from far up in the ranch country that had been bit by a rattlesnake. The child was ill and delirious. The doctor couldn't save him at this point. Arelias took turns sitting with the boy, and towards morning the child died.

About that time I went into hard labor, and Dr. Liken soon delivered a a baby girl. She weighted eight pounds and had lots of flaming red, curly hair. Arelias was pleased, and said his mother had been red headed. We named her "Elvina" after my mother.

I didn't get along very well for a day or two, and nearly wound up with infection. The doctor finally rinsed out a portion of afterbirth with very warm water and Lysol. After that I got along fine, and the baby was a chubby little dear with creases in her arms who gained daily.

Mrs. Read came to visit me and see the baby one afternoon while I was still at Mrs. Sheffield's. I had met her only once before when she was up at Buzzard's Roost that summer. She brought me two cut glass bottles, and confided, "I noticed that you and Mr. Berry don't drink coffee, and I'm going to give you these two bottles to use for milk and water at your table."

I always treasured the bottles, and years later gave them to Elvina. I never got a chance to know Mrs. Read much again, because they returned east after that.

THE SODDIE ON OUR CLAIM

Dad and Arelias worked on the new sod house on our claim whenever they could that summer, but they had to put up hay in the valley and on the river, so it was late fall before we moved in. Arelias rented an island in the North Platte River east of Lonergan Creek from Manse Sheffield for winter. He and Dad put up the hay on it, and then he wintered our cows with Dad's on the island until he had fed up the hay. He moved them all up on the creek then for calving.

We lived in Mom and Dad's house on Lonergan that winter, and they lived in the soddie that Dad had built on a quarter section of land he claimed down by the river. After the Kincaid Law of 1904 was passed, Dad was able to claim an additional three quarters of land besides the claim on Lonergan. Just before Letha and Ed married, Letha and we other girls had helped him clear the willows and brush from some ground along the river. Dad sowed alfalfa there, and built the soddie nearby. Before we were married, we girls often stayed down there during the summer.

About this same time Dad claimed another quarter section of pasture land adjoining the Lonergan claim as well. Later, when Eva was eighteen years old, she filed a Kincaid claim on a section of land not far from Arelias's claim. Here again Dad planted alfalfa. He built a little shack on it where Eva and some of the others stayed a few days every so often. Dad bought Eva's claim after she proved up on it, as well as one more section of pasture land at the head of Lonergan Creek, so that his holdings totaled about three sections all together.

We moved back to the new sod house on our claim after calving was over that spring. It was 1908, and Elvina was about eight months old. The soddie was built on a low rise to the west of a wet meadow in a valley only a few miles from Lonergan. There was a windmill south of our sod house and the yard was fenced so that the tank could be used from three sides. We got water for the house from the mill, and water for the chickens from the tank in the yard. The horses could come into the corral for water, and the cattle could water from the pasture to the west.

There was a shed for the buggy, and they built it with doors that closed with a notch at the top for the buggy tongue. There was a small barn for a horse and a milk cow, and a chicken coop in the yard.

There were no trees, but a large ridge of hills to the northwest provided some shelter from the wind and weather. Straight west were more choppy little hills, and south the sandhills rolled toward the rocky breaks of the North Platte River valley. That first year after we moved in we found that the soil in the yard on the little hill by the soddie wasn't suited for gardening. After a summer of work I had enough vegetables for one kettle of stew. Otherwise, we got along just fine, and Arelias was getting a good start in cattle and horses.

He ran some of his cattle on the Reserve. The southern Reserve boundary was only a few miles north of our place, and several of the ranchers Arelias worked for at Hyannis hired him to also look after their cattle on the Reserve. He did a lot of horse trading, and sometimes I wasn't best pleased with the results. We viewed horses much differently because he could ride or drive any horse regardless of its training or disposition. He was inclined to put any two horses together and consider them a team. Well, that wasn't the way we had done at home when I was working with Dad in the hay field.

Dad had a new project by this time. He was no longer putting up the hay along the river valley. William Paxton died in 1907, and they were now selling the valley land he had owned. The town of Keystone was platted, and lots there sold briskly. Several stores started up in Keystone, and it was soon a village. When the Union Pacific built a branch line up the North River Valley, Dad contracted to build a portion of the grade in our neighborhood. He hired a crew of men with teams and grading equipment to build the rail bed.

Then Dad got another one of his grand ideas. He decided to build a dam at the head of Lonergan to make a fish pond. As usual he directed the work, and his crews moved dirt to his design, and first thing you know, he had his fish pond. He stocked it with trout, and everyone around thought it was a wonderful thing. One time Jim McGinley, Charles Searle, and an order buyer from Omaha rode by on horseback and decided to swim their horses across it. That is not quite as simple as it seems, according to Arelias. Anyhow the Omaha man fell off his horse and drowned. Dad had a head gate in his dam that he opened to drain the pond so the body could be recovered.

Our old neighbor, LeMoyne Jacobs, not only promoted the railroad's coming up the valley, but he donated a plot of his own land for a town site. The town was officially surveyed and laid out in 1911, when it was named "LeMoyne" after Mr. Jacobs. (Eventually the town name was simply spelled "Lemoyne".) It was located just east of where Lonergan Creek ran into the North Platte. The Union Pacific Railroad soon located stockyards and a freight and passenger depot at Lemoyne.

It seemed good to have a home of our own, although we had to work hard. We were young and strong, and ready to face whatever life had in store for us. We were a good team. I helped him any way I could, and Arelias often helped me with the supper dishes or the baby. He could bake biscuits as good as mine.

We were so isolated that few people came that way. When Arelias was away I had to stay alone with the babe. She was lots of company, but evenings when she was asleep the time went slow. I had no phone or newspaper. Early one morning I woke up to the bawling of cattle. When I got up to see what was the matter, I found I was sick and dizzy. It was barely daylight, and I took some medicine I happened to have and went back to bed with the baby. About nine o'clock I was able to catch a saddle horse and ride out to see about the cattle. I left Elvina asleep in bed. It almost makes me sick now to think of what might have happened to her and me, but God kept us safe. In November of 1908 Arelias had to go up to Hyannis to move some cattle. He was going to be gone several days, and he hired a neighbor, Dan Slack, to come over and tend our livestock each day. By this time he had a stud horse that he kept in the corral. The horse was difficult to handle, and I didn't like him a bit. One day after Arelias had been gone several days, Slack came to the door and told me he had to leave at once because of some emergency. "Berry will be no doubt be back this evening, " he said, "So you won't be needing me any more."

I wasn't at all sure about that, but the man literally walked away without further comment. (He didn't own a horse.) Arelias did NOT arrive that evening, and the cow needed milking and the other stock needed hay. I propped the baby in the window so I could see her from the corral and went out to milk the cow. I forked some hay over the fence for the horses, fed the chickens, and got back to the house as soon as I could. Next day I was worried, and lonely.

It was Thanksgiving Day, so that afternoon I killed a young turkey, picked and dressed it, and put it in the oven to bake. Again I propped the baby in the window and went out to milk the cow. Just as I began to milk here came Arelias with another cowboy. He climbed off his horse and took my milk pail and said, "I'll finish this if you will get us something to eat right away. We expected to eat at one of the cow camps on the Reserve today and they were all empty and no supplies left on hand. We haven't eaten all day."

I was so glad to have him back, and I rushed to the house to make biscuits and fix supper. They ate every bit of that turkey, and what a Thanksgiving Day it was for me!

I was pregnant again, and by spring I was so heavy and awkward. The baby was due sometime around the first of June I thought. Arelias had to go to Hyannis again in May. He was going to help Joe Minor put some cattle out to pasture and bring 200 head of steers back to summer on the Reserve. Letha was visiting Mom and Dad down at Lonergan with her little boys, Charles and Gerald. She was expecting another baby and had come home to be with Mother. She and the boys came up to stay with me until Arelias returned.

The day I expected him home I was cooking a big meal for supper. Letha and I were talking and the kids were playing in front of the soddy, or so I thought. All at once I heard cattle bawling, and looked out the window to see the herd already coming over the nearest hill, and the children in front of the corral gate. I dashed outside to get the children out of the way and tripped over my skirt. I fell, but got up quickly as Letha came out to help me. We got the kids safely indoors just as the steers ran into the corral for water.

Arelias and two other cowboys arrived then, completely unaware of the situation. They were hungry, naturally, and we fed them at once. After supper as we finished the dishes up I didn't feel well at all, and soon I began to have labor pains. Arelias got quite excited and hitched up a team to the spring wagon rather than the buggy so they could put a feather bed in the bottom for me to lie upon. We took off for Lonergan with Letha and the children along. It was about six miles, and Arelias drove those horses pretty fast. Their hooves and the wagon wheels raised a lot of sand from the trail, and quite a bit of it settled on me in the bottom of the wagon.

Mom was already in bed when we rolled into the yard. Bea had gone to attend a party for a teacher who was leaving soon, but Eva and Kenneth were there with Dad. Mom got right up. She knew at once what was happening, and had them put me in her bedroom. My pains were coming hard and often by this time. At eleven o'clock our new little one arrived with Mother and Arelias on hand to do the necessary things. He was a son, and we named him John Karr Berry, after Arelias's father. My Texas cowboy was used to things happening suddenly and unexpectedly, so we got by very well. I sifted sand out of my hair, however, for several days.

A bad storm hit our little soddie before I got home with the children after John was born. It took one corner of the roof off, but Arelias and Dad had it fixed by the time we returned home.

The two children were so close in age that they were a lot of company for each other right from the beginning. They remained close always. The fall after John was a year old, we bought a half section of land joining our homestead. It was where the Schmidt place was, and there was a grove of cottonwood trees the Schmidts had set out twenty years earlier. The valley by the grove had been plowed and planted several times. After the rains that year the sunflowers grew up all over the old field.

We put the sideboards on the wagon and took it over to the field. I put a canvas tarp over part of it, and the children played in the wagon while I helped mow. (By that time we had two mowing machines.) The county fair was on in Ogallala at the time, and they planned to have a hot air balloon go up as part of the celebration. It was twenty miles away, but Arelias and I saw the balloon go up that afternoon above the horizon to the south.

Sometimes when Arelias shipped cattle, the two kids and I stayed alone. It took from three to four days for him to get back from Omaha. I had to leave the kids alone at times while I went to see if the windmills were o.k. and the cattle had water. I would be so anxious to get back to see if they were still all right.

One day I took the kids along to take dinner to Arelias and some men raising a windmill tower over in the valley by the grove. As I returned home the team became restless, and while I was closing a gate, they started on without me. The kids began to cry, and the horses trotted over the hill before I could catch up. I ran as hard as I could to the top of the hill, and saw the team stop at the gate near home. Vina got out and helped John out of the spring wagon, and they ran back to meet me. I was limp from fright, and how thankfully I gathered them into my arms, safe and unhurt. Always after that I wrapped the lines around the hub of the wheel so the horses couldn't leave me. Many times during those years we were on the claim Arelias would need repairs of some kind, and would ask me to go to Lemoyne for them. He'd hitch up the team while I got the kids ready to go. Sometimes I'd be in the midst of making bread and I'd just wrap up the dough and take it along. On the way down I'd stop at Mom's and leave the kids and the bread dough. When I got back to the creek with the repairs or supplies, Mom would have the bread baked, and I'd take it and the kids and head for home.

One day, when I went to Lemoyne for something, I drove the top buggy and a young team. As I reached the gate near Dad's shop, the tongue strap broke, and the buggy tongue came down on the ground. The team began to act up, and I turned their heads up hill to keep the buggy from running on to their heels as I cramped the wheels around. I held the lines with one hand, and dropped the children out with the other one. Then as I jumped out myself the team jerked the lines out of my hands and ran off. They tore up things pretty badly. They broke the tongue out in just a little ways, and then broke the doubletree and got completely away. My brother, Willard, chased them a mile on horseback before he finally caught them.

Arelias and Dad built a room on to the soddie with the lumber left from the old house on the Kingsley place. Dad finished it quite nicely inside with lath and plaster. In the mean time, I papered the rafters in the soddie with newspapers.

Elvina was a dreamy child. You really never guessed what was going on beneath those red curls. She was always afraid of spiders, and she didn't much like bugs of any kind. When she was just a toddler, I could leave a feather by the egg basket and she would stay completely away from it. I think she thought it was a spider or a bug. She liked horses and had a way with them, just like her dad. I happened to look out the window of the soddie one day toward the barn and corrals just as the horses were coming in to water. The kids were both by the corral watching. Presently the horses began chasing around inside the corral and I saw Elvina just slide off the fence on to one's bare back. My heart just about stopped, and I held my breath to see what would happen next. Well, thank goodness the horse didn't buck, and soon they began to run out of the corral. There was a pole up high above the gate, and just as that horse went beneath it, Elvina reached up and grabbed the pole and slid off his back. The others shied around her and she dropped to the ground all right.

I could see John was envious that he hadn't thought of doing it. The little scalawag thought of enough, heaven knows. There were two knot holes on the east side of the barn, and one time when Arelias had the stud horse tied in that east stall, John managed to stick a twig through one hole and tickle the horse while he looked on through the other hole. The horse went crazy and began to kick the stall to pieces. Just then Arelias came around the corner to put away a bridle and saw what John was up to. He gave John quite a swat on the back side with the reins, you can be sure.

TEXAS AGAIN

Arelias heard only occasionally from his family back in Texas. Roscoe, his elder brother, was working in the oil fields of Oklahoma and Texas. His sister, Stella, had married a man named Claude Bowden, and they lived in western Oklahoma. Arelias was concerned about his father. "I think I'll go down and bring Father up here to be with us." he said. I had still never met or become acquainted with any of his people, but I stayed at home looking after the homestead that trip. A fourteen year old boy named Charlie Nielson stayed and helped with the horses and the chores while Arelias was gone to Texas. It was sad though. When Arelias got to Texas, he and his father completely missed each other. The old man traveled about a great deal, and somehow he and Arelias boarded separate trains going in opposite directions, and passed each other during the night, without realizing how near they had been. Time ran out, and Arelias had to come back without even seeing his father.

Later, in November of 1912, he received word of his father's death in a hotel fire at Sandia. His brother, Roscoe, wrote a lengthy letter and spoke darkly of conspiracy and foul play. Arelias decided to investigate, and this time he wanted me to accompany him and meet his kinfolk. We left the two children with Mom and Dad on Lonergan and boarded the train for Omaha and Kansas City at Ogallala.

Ad and Ethel took their small son, Thad, along with us on the trip as far as central Oklahoma where Ad's parents and brother, Jeff, were spending the winter. Thad was only about six years old at the time, and I remember how he embarrassed Ethel by playing with the ice in his glass in a restaurant in Kansas City.

Ethel was always so proper. The night we left we were all on the sleeping car. There was a bathroom for women on one end of the car and one for men at the other end. The next morning Ethel got up and headed for the bathroom at the wrong end for her. Arelias and I were looking out of our compartment and I started to call her back, only he nudged me and shook his head with mischief in his eyes, so I kept quiet. Pretty soon she came back with a red face. "Just shut up!" she said to Arelias. "I don't want to hear one word out of you."

The Patricks left us in Oklahoma, and we went on to Duncan, Oklahoma, to visit Stella and Claude Bowden. How glad Arelias and Stella were to be together again! They were always close, and he always wanted to look after her any way he could. I remember most how bad the water was at Duncan. Stella put ice in the drinking water and then it didn't seem quite so bad, but it wasn't like the water I was used to in Nebraska.

We traveled next to Bowie, Texas, and there I met quite a number of the Berry kinfolk. I never could remember their names. I had never seen them before, and never saw them again. Everyone was talking and laughing and having a big time. I don't remember much of what was said. One of the men said, "Look at Edith blush! Haven't seen anybody blush for a long time."

Roscoe Berry arrived that night, and the next morning he came in to see Arelias and me. He looked quite different than Arelias. He was shorter and more nervous, and he looked even older than he was. Well, you know he had been knocking around for a good many years by that time. I never saw much of him, although later on he did visit us when he went to work in the Wyoming oil fields. He told Arelias their father had been shot in the midst of the fire, and that he suspected Emma South Berry, their step-mother of arranging the whole thing.

After that Arelias decided to go at once to Sandia and learn for himself what had happened the night his father died. Before he and I boarded the train to go to Sandia, he borrowed a revolver, and that night he slept with it under his pillow. It was the first time he had carried a hand gun since we were married, and I found it very disturbing. Texas seemed much less civilized than Nebraska, and as we traveled south across its flat distances I found the landscape monotonous and boring.

That trip to Texas was about the first I had ever made, and although I enjoyed the adventure, sometimes I longed for a scene more familiar. When at last we reached Sandia, I found it a raw, ugly place with few trees and even fewer other comforts.

Arelias immediately sought out the sheriff to ask about his father's death. The sheriff answered very frankly, and produced the partially burned hat J.K. Berry had been wearing. The hat had a bullet hole and blood on the crown. I can still remember Arelias holding the hat and poking his finger through the bullet hole while the law officer explained the circumstances of J.K. Berry's death. The hotel was on fire, and everyone was outside, when Berry decided to go back after some of his possessions. He somehow got to the second floor and all at once flames were all around him. It became obvious no one could get the old man out of the inferno, and then the sheriff answered the frantic pleas to shoot and end the burning man's agony.

Arelias thought the matter over and accepted the sheriff's story. He was quite satisfied to let this chapter end. Next we visited his stepmother and half sisters. I didn't like his stepmother a bit. Arelias decided it best to sign over what little property remained in his father's name to Emma's children before we departed.

Once more we boarded the train, and this time headed for the Texas Gulf Coast. At Corpus Christi we both saw the ocean for the first time in our lives. We waded into the water like children, and collected shells to take home as souvenirs. I enjoyed this part of the trip very much.

After Corpus Christi we went to San Antonio to see the Alamo. It was very important to Arelias, but I couldn't get too excited over it. It didn't seem to me that the building had ever even been finished. It was kind of an adobe stockade, just like it had been during the famous battle. I didn't know much about it of course. We went into a saloon and souvenir shop nearby. There was an enormous rattlesnake skin on the wall that I found really more interesting than the Alamo.

Once more we boarded the train, this time for Denver. And once more we seemed to travel across the endless plains of Texas forever. I asked, "Will I get to see the mountains?"

Arelias replied, "Yes, when we get to Clayton, New Mexico. I rode there one summer."

The sun was already low in the sky when we first sighted the mesas along the Texas-New Mexico border and the distant peaks of the Sangre de Cristo range. "I have gathered cattle off that." Arelias said as he pointed toward a large mesa in the distance. Meanwhile, the train had slowed to a creeping pace. Heavy rains had washed out some of the track ahead. Darkness came before we reached the mountains, but then all night long we traveled north through the Rockies.

In the morning at first light, I was looking out the window for my first sight of them. Oh, they were so pretty! There were the peaks with the sun glinting on them and just in front there was the nicest little lake. But we were soon in Denver, and we only saw the mountains such a little bit before we boarded another train for Ogallala.

Mom and Dad met us in Ogallala, and were we glad to see the kids again! They were fine of course, and it was good to be with the folks and see Lonergan Creek and the familiar hills once more. I remember that John had played north of the house at having a "shop" there, and they had a sign on the side of Mom's house that said "Blacksmithing Done Here". We all returned to the soddie on our claim that evening and found Charlie Nielson still there, and everything all right.

1913

Spring seemingly arrived early in 1913. We were full of plans and expectations that year. We had decided to build a new home in the valley on the Schmidt place. There was a grove of full grown trees there and we thought it a beautiful setting. In March Arelias and the men he hired began to scrape dirt where the house was to be, and prepare for the foundation. It was warm, and when he came home to the soddie that evening, he said he noticed the grass was beginning to come in the low places.

Arelias told me to draw up plans for the house, and he would build the barn to suit him. I drew a great many plans before I settled on one. There was to be a cellar under one corner of the house, and they dug a hole for it when they were scrapping the dirt and preparing the foundations.

On the 13th of March it looked like a storm, and when it began to mist, Arelias and the hired man gathered the cattle into the grove on the Schmidt place. It soon changed to snow, wet and heavy as only it can be in March. Then the wind began to blow. By morning it was a raging blizzard, and through the windows of our soddie you couldn't see ten feet.

All day the storm went on, and gradually it got much colder. By late afternoon the wind whipped the snow into a fine powder that made it impossible to see or even breathe if you were out in it. A.B. wanted to go to the barn and the corrals to see how the saddle horses and the milk cow were getting along. I begged him not to go because I feared he would get lost, but he and the hired man set out together, and followed my clothes line west to the fence, and then followed it to the mill and the corrals. By that time Arelias could hear the milk cow wheezing, and although he couldn't see her, he found her by the sound. Her nostrils were almost covered by the ice and snow. He managed to clear the cow's face so she could breath better. One cow and calf were in the old shed. They were completely buried as the shed was blown full of snow. He dug the cow out next day, but the calf was dead. The horses were all right, but he turned them loose out of the barn because the barn was filling up with snow. Somehow he found his way back along the fence and back to the house. When they came in I could see their faces were frost bitten, and I gathered up slush out of the snow I was melting on the stove and put it on their faces to help thaw them out.

The storm delayed our building plans for a month. The hole for the cellar was completely filled with snow, and then when the snow melted it was full of water. Drifts of snow were everywhere for a long time that spring. Everywhere the fences were covered or down, and the cattle could get out by walking on the drifts over the fence. For that matter you could drive a team and buggy over the drifts and not have to open a gate.

Naturally there was a lot of fence to fix that spring along with all of the other work. I particularly remember one fencing expedition when we were still living on the claim. Arelias bought a new horse, and since I was going to town that day, he hooked the new mare up with another horse for me to drive. The kids and I took off for Lemoyne. Arelias took another team and the wagon to go fix fence. We hadn't driven far when I heard and saw a rattlesnake alongside of the trail. I promptly struck at the snake with the buggy whip. We called that new mare Fanny, and what we didn't know about her was that she had been whip broke. When I lashed at that snake with the whip, that horse threw a fit. She reared up and came down on the buggy tongue and broke it, and we were in trouble.

I hollered at Arelias, and for a wonder he heard me. He left the team and the fencing wagon and ran down the hill to where I was. He got the horses quieted down and unhitched them, and by that time his team had turned the wagon around, and here they came back down the hill. The kids and I decided to stay home that day and not go to Lemoyne. Furthermore, we were all mighty careful with a whip around old Fanny after that. The thing that really bothered me, though, was that the rattlesnake got away.

Arelias hired Oscar Samuelson to build the house and barn, and when the lumber yard in Lemoyne sent word that a car load of lumber was in for the house, Arelias took Oscar down to inspect it. After he looked it all over, Oscar shook his head and told Arelias that most of the wood was fir rather than pine and would not be fit for anything but a little trim. Arelias refused it then and told Tom Dutch, who was managing the yard for J.W. Welpton, that he wanted number 1 pine lumber, and would accept nothing else.

"I'll be sending men and wagons down for the lumber, and if you send them back with something unacceptable, I won't pay for it, and you'll have to come get it", he told Dutch. In consequence Oscar said our house and barn were constructed of the best materials he had ever handled.

We moved into the new house in the fall, and for the first time we were where Elvina could attend school. There was a little country school house straight north of us about two miles. Mary Sanders was the teacher, and she only taught for three weeks. She was about 18 years old, and I suppose that she wasn't used to living out in the hills, and it seemed awfully lonesome. Not only that, she was in love with a railroad man, and wanted to get back where she could see him sometimes.

So Vina only went to school 3 weeks that first year. However, she already knew how to read, and she read anything we had to read. The following year we got another teacher and Vina went to school the full term.

In 1914 the Forest Reserve area up north of us was finally declared open to Kincaid claims. There was a lottery drawing at Hyannis for the claims, and very soon a flood of new people moved in there. The days of the open range and the cow camps there were over, and those outfits that had any of it fenced had to go in and remove their fences.

After the haying was over in 1914 we had a big barn dance there at our new headquarters. It was quite a gathering. Most of my family came, as well as most of Lemoyne and our neighbors, and a lot of the folks Arelias had known in the Reserve cowcamp days. The Lanka brothers and Joe Monhart played violins part of the time for the dance. They were new settlers on the Reserve.

Charlie and Oscar Samuelson also played for the dance. They had to ford the North Platte river, and they got mired in quick sand and nearly lost one of their horses. They forded in a different place when they went home. Quicksand was always a danger along the North River.

Afterwards the kids all slept in the haymow of the barn. Vina was with Bertha and Letha, and to my horror it shortly turned out that somehow all of them had picked up head lice. I had some kind of patent shampoo on hand that was supposed to deal with such things, and I poured it on Vina's hair and wrapped her head in a towel and left it there for quite a while. Then I rinsed it all out and washed her hair in the usual way. This did the trick. Vina's hair was very long, and quite heavy and curly as well, so it is a wonder I was able to get rid of the head lice without cutting her hair off.

My sister Eva married Charlie Samuelson at the Congregational Church in Ogallala. Dad was on hand, but Mother was out west to visit her brother and his family. Eva cried at the last minute because Mother couldn't be there, and Dad wished he had sent for Mother. I remember Charlie's mother saying, "Well, he was determined to marry one of you girls. If Eva hadn't consented, I do believe he would have asked Bea."

Charlie Samuelson built a house on his land south of the North Platte just west of Lemoyne. He and Eva worked so hard. Charlie had gone to an agriculture school in Sweden, and he knew a lot about plants and crops and trees. He planted several kinds of fruit trees in an orchard, and even had a vineyard of grape vines that he had developed himself. All of it flourished.

Dad went on a bear hunt with Dr. Likens up into Wyoming about this time. He enjoyed the trip immensely, and was quite happy that he got a bear before he returned home. They killed it in a wooded area, and in order to get it out over the downed timber, they had to carry the bear with its feet tied over a pole that they carried over their shoulders between them. Dad had the hide and head made into a rug. I can't think what ever became of it.

Bea was sixteen, and the only one of us girls left at home now. Elsie had married Henry Pope in Chadron in 1909. Henry was a partner in the meat market at

Chadron with Ed Kurkowski, and Elsie met him when she went up to visit Letha and Ed. Dad and Mother and the three at home——Willard, Bea, and Kenneth——went to Oregon to visit Uncle Lee and see Mom's father, Grandpa Devine.

Arelias and Ed Kurkowski looked after things on the creek that winter. Dad had bought a bunch of old cows, and A.B. and Ed had quite a time before spring. Several of them died. A.B. kept one head to show Dad when he and mother finally got back. There were very few teeth in that head. Arelias said, "If only he had consulted me when he bought them."

Letha and Ed lived in Dad and Mom's soddy on the river that winter. That spring they invited Arelias and me down to dinner one day. I was pregnant again, and that morning I went to get cream and butter from what we called "the cooling room". It was a cement walled room beneath the cistern by the windmill north of our new house. They built the cistern overhead so there would be water pressure to pipe the water into the house. The space below the cistern was dark and cool, so I kept the milk, eggs, cream, and butter there. As I stepped out with cream and butter in my hands, I caught my foot in a flounce on my petticoat. I fell, and I was quite disgusted over spilling the cream, but I thought no more about it at the time.

We went on to dinner at Letha and Ed's, and as I got into the buggy to come home I felt a sharp pain. We stopped at Mom and Dad's, and picked up Bea. (She and Mother had just gotten back from California.)

We all went home and just as Bea and I were doing up the supper dishes I began to have hard labor pains. Arelias hurried back to Lonergan to phone for a doctor. The only one he could get was Dr. Murdoch, who was new in town then. Dr. Murdoch came right out, but by the time he saw me, I had miscarried. He said I would have to be curetted, and he did it right there and then without any anesthetic. It was very painful, but I recovered all right.

Not too long after that Dr. Murdoch operated on Bill Lake's wife for appendicitis in Edna and Charlie Richard's house. They hung clean sheets all around the kitchen so he could operate on the kitchen table. Mrs. Lake recovered all right, too.

JOHN, HORSES, AND A CHURCH

For years the Searles always drove cattle by our place to take them to and from summer pasture on the Reserve. Somehow they always managed to arrive at meal time—-usually supper so they could stay the night as well. I would always have to scurry around and find enough food to cook at the last minute. There would be a couple of Searle brothers and two or three other men. Several times they brought Ed Searle's youngest kid, Rector, along. Seemed like he often exposed my kids to illness. Once he had whooping cough, and John caught it, and several times it was a cold or something.

I recall a time I was short of meat because the Searle outfit had arrived unannounced as usual. I was going out to shoot a rabbit to add to the skillet for supper. Rector was old enough to shoot by this time, and he offered to get the rabbit for me. I gave him the .22 and one shell. (That is all I needed to get a rabbit.) He must have been a fairly good shot, because he came back with a rabbit.

Funny thing. I met one of the Searle women once when we were at the fair in Ogallala. Arelias introduced me and happened to mention that we hadn't eaten yet. That woman looked rather vague and said, "Well, there is a tent here some place where the Ladies Aid are selling food. You might get something there." I was pretty disgusted after all the meals I had fed her men folks.

Growing up with sisters did not prepare me for raising a son. Brother Willard was enough younger than me that I must not have noticed his antics—-Mother told me that he had plenty of close calls and narrow escapes. Anyhow I little knew how daring and reckless John was going to be. He never seemed to be afraid of anything—-even those things that it would have been wise to fear, such as the stud horses A.B. always had around the barn and the ranch. Stallions are by nature unpredictable, mean of disposition, and hard to manage.

It is hard for me now to remember when John couldn't ride a horse. Seems like he was riding alone almost as soon as he could walk. I suppose he was actually older than THAT. Still, when it came to horses he was certainly like Arelias, and he soon rode all kinds of horses and even the wild ones. He learned that trick Arelias knew of climbing on an unbroke horse while it was tied down and staying when it was turned loose in such fashion that there was no way the horse could get at him. Arelias claimed it was how the Indians broke horses. Well, maybe the Comanche did it that way. It seemed mighty foolhardy to me.

I tell you I did a lot of worrying about the two of them and horses. John was only about eight years old when a horse got spooked in the corral one day while John was riding him. The horse bucked John off, but his foot caught somehow in the stirrup and then the horse dragged him around the corral until Arelias caught it. John had a broken arm and a lot of bruises and scrapes, and it is a miracle he wasn't killed.

Another time Arelias sent John out to bring in the horses from the pasture. He was older by this time, but still just a boy. I fixed supper and he still hadn't come in, and I began to be worried. Arelias and the other men sat down to eat. Arelias said, "The horses must have gotten out or John would be back by now." He wasn't worried, but I was, and while they were eating I walked out to the corral and listened. Pretty soon I could hear horses galloping and then as they came over the hill I heard John shout at them, "Hyahh, Hyahh, get out of here or I'll knock —— out of you."

Arelias had a good mare that he bred to a Hambletonian stallion. Her colt was really a nice one and Arelias called it Tommy. The next year or so the mare had a full brother to that colt and we called it Comet. Tommy and Comet proved to be a pair of the best horses we ever had. They were gentle, intelligent horses that you could do almost anything on. John broke Comet, and Arelias gave the horse to him. Elvina often rode Tommy and so did I.

Both Elvina and John rode together and with Arelias a lot. We had dogs, and they often went along with the kids. I remember one time Elvina and John were riding Tommy and Comet, and they had a mighty wild chase with the dogs after a coyote. The only thing they had along to kill the coyote with was a pair of fence pliers. They took turns throwing the fence pliers at the coyote. The coyote kept running, and one would keep on chasing while the other climbed off and picked up the pliers again. They eventually got him.

One summer Arelias sent me down to Lemoyne for a new hay rake. It had come in on the train to the lumber yard there. I had John along. They had the rake all put together and ready to go. As the clerk hitched it behind the team and wagon I was driving, the horses began to fret and fidget—they were a typical Flying X team—and I had all I could do to keep them in hand. The man who hooked up the rake stepped back a ways and said, "All right, Mrs. Berry, I believe that should do it." I gave the horses a little slack, and boy, they took off. John was facing the rake, and as we went across the track at a very fast pace he said, "You ran over that man with the rake wheel, Mom." Well, I was real sorry about that, but I couldn't even look back by that time, let alone turn the team around. They were headed for home, and I could see it was going to be a fast trip.

When Mother and Dad went out to LeGrande, Oregon, to visit Grandfather Devine, Dad wanted to see the country so they took their tents and camping gear. They spent most of the summer seeing Oregon. They traveled south into California and Mother got terribly sick along the way. Evidently she caught some kind of disease from the wild game she cleaned to cook. (Dad was of course living off the land as usual by shooting wild game to eat.) By the time they got to California he needed to come home and see about things, so he left her with Bea, Willard and Kenneth to spend some time with relatives there while he went home on the train. Mom sold the tents and camping equipment and then she also came home with the kids on the train.

After that they began to think of re-locating in a warmer climate. They rented a house in Redlands, California, during the winter and put Kenneth, Willard and Bea in school there.

I took Elvina and John out to California for a visit when Vina was about seven years old and John was five. We went down to Long Beach to see the ocean, and both kids loved it. Next day back at Redlands John said "I want to go down and see those big waves come in and fall over backwards."

I was pregnant, and Arelias told me to go visit the folks while I had a chance before the baby came. (It was due early in the next year.) I put Elvina and John in school for a while in Redlands. John had SUCH an imagination. He'd come home and tell me the wildest tales about seeing a snake THIS big on the way home or whatever. Elvina asked me one day without any expression on her face, "How come I walk along right beside him, and I never see these things?"

Dad had a car by then and he took us all around to see the country and visit some of his relatives who lived there. One night I returned after one of these journeys feeling ill. I went to bed, but later got Mother up because I was having pains. She sent for a doctor, and soon the baby arrived, much too soon. It was a little boy, stillborn. I grieved over losing the child, and deeply regretted being so far from Arelias. As soon as I had recovered, we boarded a train for home.

We all joined together to organize a Presbyterian Church in Lemoyne in 1914 but at that time we had neither a building or a resident pastor. Sometimes they would send us a preacher from Sutherland or North Platte. He would arrive on the train, and spend several weeks with the Lemoyne people. We all took turns boarding him at our homes.

One preacher came from somewhere back east——Rhode Island or Philadelphia or somewhere like that——and it was my turn to keep him. It was before we had a car, so I took a team and buggy to Lemoyne and brought the preacher home. Since he was an easterner, and not used to driving horses at all, let alone a team of A.B.'s horses, I drove, and when we got to the home valley, I handed the preacher the lines to hold the team while I opened the gate.

Bill Lake and two or three other men were working for us putting up the hay in that valley——it was mid-summer——and it never occurred to me that they would take a dislike to the preacher because he let me open the gate. Goodness knows, I opened the gate many a time all by myself or with the kids. The preacher hadn't ever opened a barbed wire gate, either, so I didn't figure this was the time for him to begin. He DID manage to hold the team 'til I could get the gate shut and return to the buggy. I could tell he was really nervous about those horses, because they didn't exactly stand still during that time.

The hired men watched all this from their mowers and rakes across the valley, and later at supper when I introduced the minister, they were quite respectful and polite. However, I had to fix a bed for the preacher in the bunk house that night, and I have always suspected those men of some kind of mischief, because next morning the preacher did not appear for breakfast. When I asked the men about it they all claimed to know nothing of his whereabouts. Not only did he not come to breakfast, we found his tracks on the trail headed for Lemoyne, and later we found he had boarded an eastbound train from Lemoyne. He never returned.

The hired men looked rather smug to me, and John looked wise as only a kid can when he knows something he's keeping secret. I decided not to ask any questions because it was obvious Arelias was amused and wasn't going to say anything either. Years later I learned that those men told the preacher that one of them was an Indian whose family was killed at the Battle of Wounded Knee. They said for the preacher not to be alarmed if the Indian got up in his sleep and did a war dance, and on no account to try and wake him or startle him in any way. Later on the "Indian" did a wild dance across the beds while swinging a corn knife.

The Rev. L. Branham came to Lemoyne after that and appointed a committee to raise funds to build a church. We all liked Branham a lot. He and his wife were both good, neighborly people. The Lemoyne congregation provided a house for the Branhams. It was always called "The Manse". Sometimes when we didn't have a preacher other people rented it for a short while. In 1919 we finally had enough money to begin construction of a church building. It was finished and dedicated in May of 1920. We got the old Ogallala fire and curfew bell to mount for our church bell.

It started to rain a lot about 1914. The wet meadow in the valley where we built the soddy began to have water in the middle of it all of the time. First it was just a pond, but gradually the water raised, and soon the west end had quite a lake. As a couple more wet years passed there was a sizable lake in the east end as well, and soon the water rose enough to connect the two.

Dad and Willard decided the lake was going to be there permanently, so they stocked it with fish. They went up to Three Mile Lake in the Sandhills in Dad's old T-Ford and collected a lot of bullheads in a tank they strapped to the running board. All the way back to the ranch Willard pumped air into the tank with the tire pump to keep the fish alive. Then they emptied them into our lake. In this fashion they also stocked the lake with black bass from Petersons' Pond where Dad and Mother were living in the summer time. Eventually they also stocked some blue gills, sunfish, and crappie. It wasn't long before we could go fishing in the lake and come home with quite a mess of fish. I spent many wonderful hours fishing on that lake. It was something I really loved to do.

OUR FIRST STUDEBAKER

We had a big get together near the end of 1915 before Mother and Dad left for California that winter. Dad wanted to have our picture taken while we were all together. We had one picture of Mom and Dad and us nine kids all together. Then we had a picture of Mother and Dad and all the grandchildren together. There were seventeen grandchildren now. Letha and Ed Kurkowski had four; Charlie and Edna, three; Ad and Ethel, two; Arelias and I, two; Elsie and Henry, four; and Eva and Charlie, two.

(W. P. Stansbery family 1915 – Letha, Edna, Ethel, Edith, Willard, Elsie, Eva, and Bea; Kenneth standing between Mom & Dad (W.P. and Elvina).)

Doc Watkins located in Cambridge, Nebraska, after he became a veterinarian. He and Arelias remained very good friends, and the two of them would get together whenever they could. Cars were becoming part of life everywhere, and Watkins became a dealer for Studebaker in 1915. He talked Arelias into buying one, and they set out for the factory in South Bend, Indiana, to drive two Studebakers back to Nebraska. My brother, Willard, and another man from Cambridge went along. Come to think of it, I guess none of them really knew how to drive a car.

There wasn't much of a road yet here in the west end of Nebraska, and I reckon even most of the roads in the east were not paved. They got the two cars as far as Omaha without any trouble. Just outside of Omaha near Gretna Arelias was driving, and he turned a corner too sharply going a little too fast. The car upset, and Doc Watkins looked back to see it upside down with the horn stuck and making an awful din. I guess those cars were pretty heavy and sturdy, for A.B. and Willard climbed out, not too much the worse for it. Somehow they got the car turned over on its wheels again, and headed home. Doc Watkins left them somewhere near Kearney to go to Cambridge.

About September of 1916 Arelias and I decided to take the Studebaker and go on a trip with Walt and young Harry Haythorn up into the mountains of Wyoming. Cy Kelly and Gordon Jewitt had ranches in

(Stansbery grandchildren in 1915 – Back row: Charles Kurkowski, W.P. Stansbery, Gerald Kurkowski, Letha Richards, Bertha Richards, Thad Patrick, Elvina Stansbery, Elvina Berry, John Berry. Front row: Ethel Kurkowski, Violet Samuelson, Walt Samuelson, Helen Kurkowski, Alice Pope, Della Patrick, George Pope, Lorna Richards. Joseph Pope and Fielding Pope are in the middle. There were eighteen more grandchildren born subsequent to this photograph.)

Wyoming by that time, and we decided to visit them and see the mountains. We left Vina and John with Eva and Charlie and headed west with the Haythorns from Ogallala. Arelias and I were in the Studebaker, and the Haythorn brothers, Walt's wife of a year or so, Hazel Mentor Haythorn, and her brother, "Beans" Mentor, were along in Walt's new Cadillac.

It began to rain as we drove along, and when we got to Sidney we decided to set up camp for the night at the fairgrounds. Arelias and I stopped downtown to buy a few things at the grocery store, and when we tried to leave, the car wouldn't move. The axle froze and broke. (It was something those early Studebakers would do.) There was a carload of Studebakers on the railroad track at Sidney, but the dealer refused to take an axle off one of them to repair ours. Arelias went down to a blacksmith shop and found a man who said he would make one. The man said he would work that night and have it done by the next day. He did, too. The men got the new axle installed on our car, and we all took off again.

We drove and drove, and in a day or two we camped near Rock Springs at a place called Point of Rocks. The water was not good there. Seemed like I could even taste it in the coffee. Hazel was pregnant and sometimes felt sick at her stomach, so I volunteered to do most of the cooking.

We got to Pinesdale, and Arelias phoned Cy Kelly, who had a ranch somewhere near there. Kelly told us how to find him, and we drove out to his ranch. Cy's wife, Bertha, was old Doc Hollingsworth's daughter, and I remember she was dressed all in white when we got there. I had not brought any fancy clothes along because we were going to be camping, and I felt sort of shabby next to Bertha.

Later we all piled in the cars again with the Kellys to go to Gordon Jewitt's ranch near by. I can still see Jewitt's face when we drove up and he saw Arelias. "Berry!", he exclaimed and grabbed Arelias by the hand. They had been cowboys together up on the Reserve and the ranch country around Hyannis, and were they glad to be together again!

The men all made plans to go hunting up in the mountains. We left next morning and made camp near a stream. We women went along, but we stayed in camp with Beans Mentor because there weren't enough horses for everyone. Arelias and the others rode out in search of Elk to hunt. I wanted to see more of the country, so Beans and I walked out from camp a ways. There was so much downed timber, however, that we soon turned back because it was so difficult to cross.

I returned to the large teepee that the men had erected at camp and found the other women all admiring and shining their diamond rings. I figured they were trying to impress each other, so I left again. I had just stepped back outside when I heard an elk bugle. It is a sound I have never heard again, even though I have hunted in Wyoming many times.

Meanwhile, the men were supposedly out looking for elk, but they were visiting and talking so much that they never saw one. Mrs. Jewitt went out later with her little shotgun, and every so often she would blast away at something. I never knew her to actually hit anything, but she scared the squirrels and birds.

We had a lot of fun though, and I loved the mountains. Again I did most of the cooking. Hazel wasn't feeling well, and the other two women simply didn't know how to cook over a camp fire. Arelias helped me some, because of course he knew how to cook over a camp fire.

We had to head for home all too soon, and as we were driving across country somewhere in central Wyoming going towards Casper, we found a man standing beside a Model T Ford that wouldn't run. He asked us, "Do you know anything about a Ford?"

The Haythorns looked at each other and Walt said, "Why, we can BUILD a Ford." They fixed it right away, and then we drove on. At Casper we all ate in a restaurant, and I remember that Hazel was beginning to feel more like herself at last. She managed to eat a whole steak. We separated at Casper. The Haythorns were going to visit someone they knew there, but we had to be getting home.

Several months later Hazel gave birth to a baby boy at the north ranch in Arthur County where they were living. Arelias and I went up right away to see the baby, whom they named "Waldo". As we stood looking at the child in his basket, Walt asked Arelias, "Do you think he looks like me?"

Arelias got that poker faced look that he always got when he was going to say something really outrageous. "Well, no," he said, "I think he looks more like old Dave R——." (Dave R. was a local bootlegger.)

Walt got even with him years later when our daughter, Ruth, was born on the ranch in 1925. He and Hazel came to see the baby, and Walt told Arelias, "She looks just like Old John H————." (John H. was quite a disreputable character around Lemoyne.) In spite of the hardships and the many difficulties we experienced, there was a lot of fun and laughter in those years when we were all getting started.

About that time Arelias bought the Parrish place north of us. It had a fairly good frame house on it, and he got a notion to send to Oklahoma for Stella and Claude. They were pretty hard up at the time and he was sending them a little money whenever he could. Arelias told me "I'll just find another job for Charlie Nielson, hire Claude, and they can live up there on the Parrish place."

Charlie Nielson was almost like one of my own kids by that time, and I hated to see him go. However, Arelias found him a good job with George McGinley, and we sent for Stella and Claude. They arrived in May with their children, and I remember it snowed that year in May. Curtiss was their youngest. He was a little red headed toddler, and he had never seen snow before. He just had to dive out the door and run around in his bare feet! The three older children were Rufus, Homer, and Anna Mae.

The summer before the World War broke out a group of Keith County men got the idea to put on a big rodeo. They had never done that before here. They organized the Ogallala Commercial Club, and they wanted to somehow commemorate the town's history as the end of the Texas Trail. Lou Cogger from down on the Birdwood helped persuade them to put on a rodeo , and he contracted to furnish the livestock for it. They asked Arelias to be one of three judges for the bronc riding. The Commercial Club sent flyers every direction with any traveler passing through town. (The Lincoln Highway was built through Ogallala from the east that same year.)

The Round-Up took place the last of August. Arelias roped in it besides serving as a judge. Harry and Walt Haythorn and most all of the cowboys in the country were contestants. They seemed to have a lot of fun at it. My goodness, there was a crowd of onlookers! Jack Kroh, who had started a newspaper in Ogallala, estimated there were over 1000 cars in town, and several thousand of people.

They repeated the event in 1917, and that year Al Kehr, who was running a theater in Ogallala then, had someone come photograph the rodeo on a movie camera. In 1918 they put the round-up on one more time, and that year a cowboy from down south came up a couple of weeks ahead of the rodeo on the train and went around the country looking for a good horse to use in the steer roping.

His name was Jim Wilkes, and he came to our place and asked Arelias to let him try out a horse. We had a lot of horses in those days, but Wilkes immediately singled out Tommy and Comet. Wilkes rode Tommy and was immediately sure that was the horse he wanted to use in the Ogallala show. Arelias agreed to let Wilkes use the horse, and they got ready to go to the big show. Wilkes broke a rib the first day of the show, and for the remaining shows, he wore a leather brace around his middle to keep the ribs in place. I don't suppose he should have been contesting again so soon, but that never slowed up those old time cowboys.

Arelias judged the bronc riding again. He entered the steer roping, and the first two days he did well so it looked to me like he might win the title on the third day. I had watched both shows the first two days, and was really excited about the last show. That morning I looked at John, and found he was coming down with the measles. There was nothing for it but to keep him home and stay myself. I was so disappointed! When Arelias caught his steer that day, his rope broke when the steer hit the end of it. Even so, he managed to catch the end of the rope when it flew back, and as he rode on he tied a new hondo around the rope and formed another loop. (It was a thing he had learned to do in the old brush popping days in Texas.) He still caught the steer, but Jim Wilkes had better time.

At the end of the Ogallala Round-Up in 1918 a photographer took a wide angle photograph of all the cowboys in front of the grandstand. Arelias and Jim Wilkes were both in it along with the Haythorns and all of the others. It was the last rodeo in our country for several years, and the last one to have so many of the old timers in it. Years later it was very different when a whole new generation of cowboys began to put on rodeos again.

1918 Ogallala Round-Up
In line, left to right, Kildare, Hill DePriest, Chet Davis, Walt Haythorn, Ed Herron, Bert Breen, _____, Guy Davis, Ed Coates, A.B. Berry, Jim Wilkes, Myrtle Cox, Fred Cox, _____, Jim Abrian, Tom Plummer, June Chesmore, Lou Cogger, Herman Hopkins, Paul Hanson, Knight Lowe _____, Ed Carlyle, Frank Carter, Hans Peterson, _____, Arch Manso _____ Bert Sheldon, Frank Brown. In front, Lafe Luman. Background, Clarence Fisher with megaphone, Walt Nye, left, Henry Woolery, Jack Kroh, and H.R. Carlyle, to right. Rector Searle in uniform. Frank Harris on fence.

WAR AND FLU

The town of Lemoyne was getting to be quite a village by this time. The Keith County commissioners finally agreed to build another bridge across the North Platte River just west of Lemoyne. In 1917 the Bishop Construction Company came to Lemoyne to build the bridge. It was a family company. Mr. Bishop was busy elsewhere on another job, so he sent his sons and a crew to Lemoyne. He put his son, Ralph, a tough, scrappy young fellow, in charge. He and his brothers and their crew completed the bridge that same fall, and it was open to the public for travel in October of 1917.

Ralph Bishop soon began to court my sister Bea, and it wasn't long before she confided to Ethel and me that she was going to marry him. Ethel exclaimed, "But Bea, you don't care enough. I was in the clouds when I decided to marry Ad."

Bea laughed and replied, "Oh I care enough, but after the years of helping six older sisters with their kids and observing their marriages, I have my feet on the ground." Ralph and Bea were married March 8, 1919. How fortunate it was that Bea was so very experienced and practical. Ralph's work took him everywhere. When she could go with him, she did, and often kept house under very trying conditions.

Ralph's mother was a preacher for the Church of God. I remember several years later Mrs. Bishop came to visit Ralph and Bea one time when they were living in Lemoyne. I drove her through the sandhills to the ranch in our car. The weather had been dry for quite a while, and the roads were awfully sandy. I had to drive pretty fast and not let up in order to keep from getting stuck. When we got to the ranch, Mrs. Bishop told Arelias, "You've heard of heroes, well Mrs. Berry is a SHE-ro."

The United States declared war against Germany in 1917, and right away young men began to volunteer. My brother Willard soon joined the armed forces as did Charlie Nielson. Willard had quit school in California the year before, much to Mother's disappointment. An old man hired Willard to drive him on a sight seeing tour of California. Willard really got to see some country, and he told Mother it was a better education than school. Then the war began, and he volunteered.

By 1918 we were in the midst of rationing and shortages because of the war. If you bought wheat flour, you were required to take other kinds of flour in proportion. There was potato flour, rye flour, corn meal, and other grains they wanted to use instead of wheat. I would get as much wheat flour as they permitted and usually took the balance in corn meal. I could make good corn bread that Arelias and the kids would eat, but I never could make decent bread out of potato flour and some of those other grains. Seemed like the bread always turned out heavy and sort of gummy.

There was a lot of sickness that fall, and the doctors were calling it "influenza". Charlie Richards took sick in October, and died on the thirtieth of that same month. A lot of fun and laughter went out of the world with him. He and Edna's youngest child, Lorna, was only three years old. Elsie and Henry Pope were experiencing a lot of sorrow in these years also. They lost their baby daughter, Dorothy, to illness. Their next youngest child, George, died in a fire caused by playing with matches in the barn.

We rented the "Manse" that fall in Lemoyne so I could stay there during the week while Vina and John attended school in Lemoyne.

Bea took sick, and Elvina was there with her. Mother and Dad were gone somewhere. When we went to get Vina, Bea said, "I've had the flu, and I don't know what I'd have done without Vina to read to me and get things for me." Trouble was that Vina soon took sick, and shortly afterwards, John and I. Doctor Murdoch came and gave us all some medicine and said "Now, you shouldn't be here alone. Get someone to be here with you."

I sent word up to the ranch for Arelias to come, and it turned out he had gone up north to the Tuckson place to see Stella and Claude. He was renting Andy Tuckson's place at this time, and Stella and Claude were living there to look after the cattle. Arelias rode home as soon as they got word to him, and he immediately came on down to Lemoyne.

Everyone in Lemoyne was scared of the flu because it seemed to be so contagious, and it was frequently fatal. They closed the schools, and canceled all public meetings. People were afraid to be around each other for fear of being exposed to flu. I remember one neighbor lady bringing a dressed chicken to the door for us, and holding it out at arms length to avoid any more contact than necessary. A.B. was sort of offended. He said, "In Texas they wouldn't be this way." But of course in Texas they probably were that way. There had never been anything like this before in our country.

I got pneumonia and ran a terrible fever. My hair all fell out, and after that I never wore it long again. When I began to recover, we went back to the ranch, and Bea was with me for a while. Mom and Dad had gone to California for the winter just before we all got sick. I got phlebitis in one leg—I suppose because I was in bed so long. I remember that one evening at the ranch I had hot packs on that leg, and then Bea rubbed it for me. A few hours later I woke from a sound sleep with a terrible pain in my chest. Almost immediately it passed, and then I felt rather weak. Next morning Dr. Murdoch told me that a blood clot had worked loose from my leg and gone through my heart. He said it was a mighty close call. Still, I eventually recovered.

I remember the day we all got word that the Armistice had been signed and the war was over. They turned school out, and all of the kids went down and played by the lumber yard. Everybody got together and celebrated. It was the first time folks had done much socializing since the flu began. Willard and Charlie Nielson's regiments never sailed for Europe. The flu broke out then, and more men died from it than would have likely been killed at the front. Willard helped care for the sick, and although he got it, he recovered, but Charlie died. The funeral was at Big Springs, and our whole family attended.

Mom and Dad had finally decided to sell the place on Lonergan and buy a house in California. Frank and Jed Harris, two brothers from Custer County, soon agreed to buy the house and land on Lonergan Creek. Dad kept the quarter of meadow along the North River with the soddy on it, and eventually he gave it to Willard. Right away the Harris brothers began to move their wives and families to Lemoyne.

Arelias and I attended a card party in Lemoyne honoring Mrs. George Adam's birthday. They kept shifting the players around, and at one time I was seated at the same table with Jed Harris. He confided that he had never found anyone with the same birthday as his own——April 12. I told him that was my birthday and also my sister, Edna's. We laughed and said when spring came we must have another card party for OUR birthday. However, by the time April 12 came, Jed Harris had died of influenza. His brother, Arch, bought his interest in the Lonergan place from Jed's widow.

Willard came home right after the Armistice. He wrote that he could come home right away if he had fifty dollars for the train ticket. It seemed that otherwise he'd have to wait for formal discharge when the army would pay his way home. I had fifty dollars in a savings account, and I wired it to him immediately.

Willard surprised us all a year later when he married Irma Fancher of Lemoyne. She was the daughter of Frank Fancher, a Lemoyne school teacher who also owned a homestead near Lemoyne. Her brother, Richard, worked for Arelias one time for a while, but other than that we weren't acquainted with her people. Willard and I were always close, and he worked many times for Arelias. At first I found it strange to think of him grown up now with a home of his own. He and Irma began married life in the soddy Dad had built down by the river so many years ago.

FIFTEEN FLAT TIRES TO YELLOWSTONE

After Mother and Dad sold the place on Lonergan, they decided to dispose of some of their belongings. Dad went around to all of his sons-in-law and told them, "Now I'm not going to have a sale. You all need things. I'll charge you a fair price, and you can just buy them from me. A.B., you need shop tools, so you buy the forge and blacksmith tools, and so on." So that is what we all did. Arelias and I bought Dad's old roll top desk, and all of the sons-in-law bought whatever hay machinery and other equipment they wanted. Ad Patrick bought Dad's old 8 gauge shot gun that he had used so many years.

I'll never forget the Patricks and that gun. Although she grew up around it, Ethel had never shot it. None of us had. One morning after Dad sold it to Ad, Ethel noticed the blackbirds were eating her sweetcorn. She ran in the house and got the old 8 gauge shot gun, propped it up on a post, and pulled the trigger. Well, it kicked like a mule, and of course she wasn't holding it right anyway, and it just knocked her out. Ad and his men heard the shot. They came running to see what had happened, and found her lying on the ground unconscious. She came around after bit, but wasn't her arm black and blue for a spell!! I was the only one of us girls who learned to shoot a gun. Arelias taught me after we were married. He soon bought me a .22 rifle, and I would practice on rabbits and prairie dogs out in the pasture or sometimes along the road as I went to and from Lemoyne. I remember one evening Arelias came home and said, "I saw some dead rabbits along the road. They seem to have died of lead poisoning." One time I took aim at a pheasant, and just as I pulled the trigger, it turned its head, and I hit it right through the eye. Arelias showed it to Elvina and John and said, "Now THAT'S how your mother shoots a pheasant." I seemed to have a true eye with a gun just like dad, and I became a very good shot.

We bought an Oldsmobile early in 1919, and at first we liked it well enough. That summer we decided to take Elvina and John and go visit Bert and Belle Burgess, who had a ranch in the mountains of northeast Wyoming at the time. Before we set out for Cheyenne Arelias bought two new tires to carry along with us besides the ones already on the car. We took tents and camping supplies because there were few hotels or places to stay in the territory we would be going through.

By the time we reached Cheyenne the Olds wasn't working quite right, so Arelias took it to a garage for some repairs. Then we left Cheyenne on a dirt road for Chugwater. From there we angled off across the country around Casper until we came to a railroad. We followed the railroad to Moneta, a little place with stockyards and a store. Most of that time we traveled along in heat and dust where there wasn't much grass through open country. The extra tires were tied atop the trunk on the back of the car, and some place across that desolate land the tires came loose and fell off. By the time we missed them, we didn't have any idea where to go look for them, so we just kept on going. When we met someone going the opposite direction, Arelias stopped and told that person where to send the tires if he came across them, but we never heard any more of the tires again. At Moneta we left the railroad and headed north along a dirt trail towards Lost Cabin.

The country began to change as we drove into the foothills. We went up over a rocky trail into the high country and drove along streams, grassy meadows, and timber down into the Big Horn Basin. So beautiful. The more I saw of the mountains, the more I loved them. We came to Hyattville at last, and soon we located the Burgess ranch in the valley along Paintrock Creek. Believe me, those two Texans were really glad to see each other once more.

Bert hitched a four horse team to a mountain wagon with brakes on it that he hauled salt and one thing and another to his cattle on the mountains, and we loaded all our camping gear in it to go out camping in the mountains. Bert took us up to the head waters of Paintrock Creek. There were two little mountain lakes, and we camped beside the one known as Medicine Lodge Lake. The children were all along——Bert and Belle's two boys, Jinx and Russell, as well as John and Elvina. Arelias spent most of his time hunting grasshoppers for me and the kids to use as bait. Elvina landed a big trout almost as soon as she put her line in the water. I got six or eight smaller ones. How I did like to fish! For our meals we fried fish over a camp fire and made biscuits in a Dutch oven and fried potatoes to eat with them.

We camped out up there for three days, and then we went back to Bert's ranch and got ready to travel on. We planned to take the kids to Yellowstone Park to see a bear. The morning we left we had a flat tire before we got to Basin. We didn't realize it at the time, but at least one of the wheels on the Oldsmobile was sprung from our journey over rocks and rough roads. The rim was cutting the stem to the tube of the tire where it came through the wheel. However, after Arelias fixed the tire we made it on into Yellowstone without further trouble. We camped there for a few days and looked at everything. One morning a deer came right into our camp. It was a breath taking moment. They are such shy creatures, and soon it ran away in that bounding way they have. There were bears all right, and one morning we got up to find they had broke into our supplies and made off with the bacon during the night.

Elvina and I fished some more, but John was mainly interested in the big tour busses the Park Service ran for sight seeing around the park. Those busses had big steam motors, and John was wanted to know how they worked. We saw most of the many wonders of Yellowstone. It was all magnificent, and up to the time we left the park and headed home, we had a wonderful time.

At last we had to leave for home, and that was when we had a bad time. Poor Arelias. We had one flat tire after another. We finally drove the last 20 miles into Chugwater on the rim. The tire was totally ruined. They didn't have a tire there that would fit our car, but a man drove in after a while with a spare on his car that was the right size. It was used, but A.B. bought it from the man just to get out of town. We finally reached Cheyenne, and he bought two tires and prepared to pay for them by check. The owner wouldn't accept his check because it was on an out of town bank. Arelias went down to the depot to wire for money, and blessed if he didn't meet up with Cy Kelly and Ed Hayes. They came back with him and told the filling station owner that A.B.'s check was good, and Cy Kelly added, "Now listen here, if that man ever comes in here again and needs money, you let him have it and charge it up to me."

We headed for Sidney then, and before we got there, a wheel had cut a hole in a tube again. Arelias changed it, we drove on, and finally we were nearly home and going down the Cramer hill into the North River Valley when we had yet another flat—- the fifteenth one. He got out wearily to change it and said to me, "Wife, if I ever leave home in this car again any further than you can throw a rock, I want you to shoot me."

He meant what he said. He bought a Dodge Coupe soon afterwards and parked the Olds in the fence row. The weeds came up around it, and once in a while he would take a piece off it for repairs.

ELVINA: THE SCHOOL YEARS

That fall Mother and Dad left for California again. The doctor told me I should not spend the winter in Nebraska because my lungs were weak from having flu and pneumonia the winter before, so I made plans to visit them during the winter. Edna and her girls planned to accompany Mother and Dad, and it seemed we might as well send Elvina and John along to start school there. I intended to come later after I finished some chores at the ranch and had every thing ready to leave. However, the night before they were to leave, Arelias came in and said, "I just can't let those kids go that far away without one of us along. You'd better get ready and go with them." Well, I just had to fly around and gather up things. I wasn't in any way prepared, but when they left next day I was along.

Mom and Dad's place in Redlands, California, was on a big corner lot. There was a large two story house as well as an orange grove and some other fruit trees. They planted a garden and kept a few chickens. Even though the house was big, it was pretty crowded there that fall. In addition to Edna's family, and 'Vina, John and me, Dad's sister, Aunt Nan, was there, and on some weekends her son, Jay, would come down also. Kenneth was still at home and training to be a journeyman electrician.

We all liked to go down to Longbeach to see the ocean. It was nearly a hundred miles, but on nice weekends Dad often loaded us into his old car, and away we went. Besides the beach and the ocean there were all sorts of activities and amusements of one sort or another going on there. Mother particularly like to go listen to the preachers and tent speakers. There was always a big Salvation Army service that she liked to attend.

Edna got work packing oranges with a local shipping concern. I bought a second hand sewing machine so we could mend, and Edna also did sewing for people. I remember she made a nice little girl's coat for some neighbor lady. But with that many of us there, it was sometimes difficult.

I began to be quite homesick after a while. I longed for Arelias and my own house. I stayed through Christmas, but then I got ready to leave for home. It was New Years Day when I finally gathered up the kids and our things, said a loving goodbye to Mom and Dad, and boarded the train for Nebraska.

Mother sent a big jar of pear honey packed in a bucket especially for A.B. He once expressed a desire for pear honey, and said it was a sort of southern preserve or jam they made in Texas. There was a pear tree in the yard at the house in Redlands, so Mother figured out how to make pear honey, and sent us home with a large jar of it.

Arelias was waiting for us, but our train was late, and he finally checked into the hotel and went to bed. We arrived in the middle of the night and I and the kids went to the hotel, and as I wrote my name, the clerk said, "There's another Berry staying here tonight. "

I looked and saw Arelias' name and said, "That's my husband." So we went up stairs and woke him up.

Elvina finished the school year at the school near Patricks and stayed during the week with my sister, Ethel. The following year she completed the eighth grade at Lemoyne. Most of the time that year I drove the kids back and forth to Lemoyne to school. The next year Elvina began high school in Ogallala. Mr. and Mrs. Ben Carey ran a store in Lemoyne, and three of their children were high school age. Mrs. Carey decided to rent a house in Ogallala to put her kids in school and take in boarders. We decided to let Elvina stay with Mrs. Carey. Haney Carey was the same age as Elvina, and the two of them shared a room.

The next year I rented the Kluff house near Arrowsmith's home and mortuary, and put both Elvina and John in school in Ogallala. John was sixteen by the next fall, and he had a Model T runabout. He and Elvina drove to school in Ogallala each morning from the ranch until the weather got cold and unpredictable. One morning John turned a corner too short and upset the car. Elvina was pinned under it, but a driver from another car right behind them helped John lift the Ford and free her. Her back was hurt though, and often gave her trouble afterwards.

In November my sister, Ethel Patrick, and I rented the Williams house on Spruce Street in Ogallala and put John and 'Vina and Thad and Della Patrick all in school. The house was located next door to the new hotel they were building in Ogallala at the time. They ran out of funds for completing the hotel, and it was boarded up and empty that winter. Kind of spooky to be next door to it, I recall.

Our sister, Bea, also moved in with us that winter. Her little boy Kenny was just a toddler, and she was expecting another baby later on in the year. Ralph was off in Maryland somewhere building a bridge. As their children came, Bea could not always go on location with Ralph. She was a great help to us. Often Ethel and I needed to be at home out in the country, and we knew the kids were all right in town with Bea there.

We sisters always helped each other. It was one of the many lessons Mother and Dad had taught us so well. Life in those days out here in western Nebraska was not easy, but it was possible and even rewarding if a family loved each other and helped each other. Even after we were grown up and quite a ways apart at times, we cared for each other and our families, and helped one another. But Bea especially helped us all.

When Elsie's husband, Henry, took sick in 1920, she called Bea, who was in Iowa at the time with Ralph, to come help her. Kenneth was just a baby, but Bea gathered him up, climbed on the train, and went to Chadron. Elsie's husband did not recover, and after he died, Bea stayed on to help her come to grips with things. The trouble was that Henry had always taken care of all the business matters——probably because Elsie was terribly busy with five children——so she knew nothing about managing the store in town or the farm in the country. In fact, Elsie had never written a check. Bea had to show her how.

Things didn't go well for Elsie for many years after that. We all tried one way and another to assist her. She rented the farm to a tenant, and I remember once she needed a team of work horses for the farm. Arelias had a team that he thought would do, so one morning he saddled up and left our place leading the two horses towards Chadron. It was over one hundred miles across country, and it took him a couple of days, but he got the team to her.

Arelias loved all of the young cousins, and over the years so many of them stayed with us, and several of the nephews worked for him during the summers and what not. Claude and Stella's boys frequently worked for him. In fact we eventually enclosed the north porch on our house and made a bedroom in one end so we would have a place for Stella's boys to stay. Both Rufus and Homer worked for us different times. Elsie's two boys, Joseph and Fielding, spent a summer or two with us when they were about sixteen.

When Elvina was a high school senior, Hazel Haythorn came to town and rented a house to put Waldo in school. (He was in the third grade that year I think.) Hazel agreed to board Elvina and Haney Carey, and they stayed with her until Christmas. Hazel got quite sick then, and couldn't keep them after that. Haney stayed on to work for her and help take care of Waldo. Elvina and John finished out the year boarding at Robinsons'.

Both John and Elvina were good students, and Elvina finished second high in her graduating class, only a fraction of a grade point behind Doris Smith. She was also on the debating team that year in high school.

Elvina cut her hair when she was sixteen. Before that she had always worn it in long braids or curls, but short hair became the style for girls and young women in the 'Twenties. Elvina's new hair style was called a "pineapple bob". Arelias was shocked at first, but we both soon realized that for her heavy, curly hair, the short style was quite becoming.

Both kids were going to dances by this time, and I guess Arelias and I had to realize they were growing up. The dances were very different from the ones we attended before we were married. They didn't dance the old reels and quadrilles any more, and the music was not the fiddle and piano music we knew so well. We had an Edison phonograph with lots of different kinds of music on the records, and John and Elvina learned to dance to it. The dance steps were quite outlandish, some of them. I remember one in particular called the Charleston that both John and Elvina soon learned to do. They also waltzed and two- stepped, mostly to popular band music. They had several friends that they went to dances with, and always it seemed, the cousins looked out for each other—'Vina and John, Thad and Della Patrick, Violet Samuelson, Bertha and Letha Richards, and the Kurkowski cousins, Charles, Gerald, and Ethel, were all of an age.

The summer after she graduated from high school Elvina took it into her head to go visit her Uncle Roscoe in Casper, Wyoming. I didn't want her to go, but she was determined to do it, so we put her on the train at Lemoyne and eventually she got to Casper. Roscoe and his wife enjoyed having her there a lot, and she came home knowing a bit more about the Berry family. It seemed to matter a lot to her.

Arnold McKeag began to call on Elvina and take her places during their senior year in high school. He was a tall, dark young man, quiet but likable, who played football on the high school team. His parents, Mr. and Mrs. John McKeag, moved to Keith County from eastern Nebraska just before the World War. There were other young men who paid attention to her as well, but neither Arelias or I took any of them seriously yet. She seemed very young to us. We wanted her to experience a bit more of life before she married and settled down, and in the fall after she graduated we sent her to the college in Redlands, California. She stayed with Mother and Dad while she attended the college, for it was very near their home.

RUTH

Arelias and Walt Haythorn shipped dry cows together in July of 1925. The day they loaded the cattle out of the stockyards at Lemoyne, I packed Arelias's clothes and things in a satchel for him, because he was riding the caboose to Omaha with the cattle. It was afternoon when I drove to Lemoyne with the satchel, and the road down through the Harris place was fine. The train was just about ready to leave as I handed the satchel to Arelias. I stood on the south side of the tracks and waved goodbye to him as he went by on the caboose. Meanwhile, the Harris brothers let some irrigation water get away from their ditch, and it washed a gully in the road. As I was drove home I hit that ditch in the road, and it gave me an awful jolt.

I was pregnant, and the baby was due in about six weeks. I got home all right, but next day I had problems. I sent for the doctor and my sister, Ethel. They both arrived quite soon, but I didn't seem to be in labor. Nothing further happened that evening so the doctor returned to town, and I told him to phone North Platte and have a nurse come up on the train. Arelias was back from Omaha by the time the nurse arrived, and not too long after that I DID go into labor. The baby——a little girl who only weighed six pounds——finally arrived July 16 in our house there at the ranch. We named her "Ruth Aurelia".

She was a good baby, and she slept a lot. One day late that summer Mother and Dad came by to visit. Mother stayed with me, while Dad went out with Arelias and some others to do some shooting. It was quite warm, and I particularly remember how red in the face Dad was when they returned. He stood in the south porch looking at the baby, mopping his forehead, and saying, "That baby is always asleep when I see her."

Mother looked up and calmly said, "When a baby is that small, it is SUPPOSED to sleep a lot."

Soon after that Dad suffered a stroke. He was somewhat paralyzed on one side, and he walked with difficulty after that. Still, he was able to sit and visit with the family in the usual way. Letha and Ed Kurkowski sent their daughter, Ethel, to California with Mother and Dad that fall to help Mother care for Dad during winter, for Mother had her hands full keeping Dad comfortable and content, and she was getting older and less able also.

Ruth was still just an infant when Ralph Bishop was seriously injured while they were building a bridge across the Snake River in Idaho. Bea was living in Lemoyne with their three small children. Ralph was in the hospital and she knew she must go out there at once. Arelias sent Rufus Bowden to drive Bea and the kids out to Idaho, and I drove our car with Ruth on a pillow in the seat beside me.

We stayed a month so Rufus could work on the construction crew and earn a month's wages while we were there. I stayed with Bea and helped with the kids. Ralph eventually recovered, but it was a long ordeal, and afterwards he had very little sense of taste or smell. I fished in the Snake River a time or two with Lee Bishop's tackle. The river was very deep and swift; you had to keep casting. I caught Lee's artificial flies in the trees trying to cast beyond the bank, and had very little luck. Finally I caught a white miller and baited a hook with it, and right away I caught a huge trout. We ate it for lunch, and that afternoon we fished again, but no one caught anything then.

At the end of the month we left for home. Rufus drove most of the way. We stopped at Casper on the way back to Nebraska to visit Roscoe Berry. I remember that Ruth cried all night that night. The roads had been so rough and dry—-like a wash board. As we left Casper next morning it began to rain, and we soon got stuck in the mud. Shortly after we got out of that, I was driving and had a flat tire—-we had picked up a nail somewhere. We finally got home, and Rufus was exhausted. A.B. was so glad to see us. He was afraid the baby had forgotten him, because we had been gone so long. She hadn't. He held out his arms, and she went right to him.

(Ruth Berry)

Ruth was a dear little bit of a thing, and both of us enjoyed her a lot, but Arelias particularly. He simply adored that child. She was still quite small when lightning struck and killed one of the brood mares out in the pasture. Arelias gave the motherless colt to Ruth, and we named it Orphan Annie, after the comic strip in the newspapers then. We fed the colt on a bottle that summer, and then fed it sweetened mash. It was Ruthie's special pet, and there was a bond between the two that lasted until the horse grew old and died.

Even as a very small child, Ruth had a mind of her own, and she could be quite contrary. That colt liked sugar, and Ruth was always raiding my sugar bin to get lumps for Orphan Annie. I finally forbade her to get any more sugar out of the kitchen. She gave me a long look, and didn't say anything, and thereafter I didn't see her in the sugar bin any more. However, sometime later Arelias confided to Elvina that Ruth had a bucket of sugar hidden in the haymow of the barn from which she continued to provide Orphan Annie a daily nibble.

Once when she had been particularly naughty, Arelias spanked Ruth. Afterwards we looked out the dining room window and saw her standing against Orphan Annie with her arms around the colt's neck and her head against its shoulder as if Orphan Annie were her only friend in the world. Arelias felt so bad, and after that he hardly ever scolded her, much less spanked her.

My sister, Eva Samuelson, had her sixth child the same summer that our Ruth was born. She and Charlie named their little boy "Leroy", but everyone always called him "Laddie". Eva was worn out and really didn't get along well at all after Laddie's birth. By the time the kids were about three years old, and she still wasn't well, the doctor recommended she go to the mountains for a while in the summer to see if she would feel better. (Actually, with six children as close together as hers were, what she needed most was simply rest.)

Charlie couldn't leave during the summer, and I finally suggested that she and I go up to Casper, Wyoming, to visit Roscoe Berry and his wife. Elvina was home that summer, and she could cook and take care of things in the house and garden while I was gone. Arelias agreed, so Eva and I and Ruth and Laddie set out in our car. We got to Casper all right, and then decided to go up into the mountains and camp for awhile. Roscoe went with us and showed us to a camp ground near the top of Casper Mountain. It was a terrible trail road with high centers in places. On the way up my car got too hot. Roscoe told me when we came back down, I must put the car in low and keep it there 'til we reached the bottom of the mountain. I did, and we made it safely back. Roscoe grinned and said, "You're a pretty good driver, Sis."

The year Elvina attended college in Redlands, Mom and Dad decided to come home early in the spring. School wasn't over yet, and she was homesick and wanted to come too. I finally sent her a wire telling her to come with them. Imagine how surprised we were when we met the train, and found that Arnold McKeag was meeting it also. I guess when we saw how glad they were to see each other, we knew how things were going to be.

(Arnold McKeag and Elvina Berry)

Arnold McKeag worked in Porter's Hardware Store after he and Elvina graduated from high school. He bought a green Chrysler coupe, and he drove out to see Elvina frequently on weekends. I remember one time he took her to a dance, and after he brought her home, he headed back to Ogallala. He was sleepy, and as he drove across the flat on the W—— place, he went out of the trail and into a mud hole. And was he stuck! He finally had to walk up to the W——' house and get the old man up to come pull him out. Arelias and I were quite disgusted when we learned of the incident later, because W—— charged Arnold FIVE DOLLARS to pull him out. The road went right by us, and all those years we helped plenty of people out of mud, snow, and sand and never once charged them for anything. Poor Arnold, he made it home about the time he had to leave for work the next morning, and he said afterwards he was just about asleep on his feet most of the next day.

Ruthie made friends with Arnold right off, and she would run ahead of Elvina to meet him at the door sometimes. One day she flipped up her skirt and said, "Look at my new pink panties." I remember Arnold blushed furiously, but he admired them, nonetheless.

Arnold and Elvina wanted to get married. Arnold soon talked to Arelias about their plans. Arelias approved of Arnold, and as they talked things over he smiled and said, "Elvina likes to go to church. I hope you'll see that she can sometimes." I suppose it seemed a strange request to Arnold at the time, but he said he surely would. He did, too.

They were married on April 27, 1929. It was Arnold's 21st birthday as well. The wedding took place in our home there on the ranch. Elvina and I shopped in Ogallala and found a beautiful dress for her to wear. It was silk crepe in a sort of cream color the sales lady called "champagne". It looked wonderful with Elvina's red hair and fair complexion. We had the minister from the Lemoyne church, and a few relatives that included our family and the Patricks as well as Arnold's parents and his younger sister, Hazel. John was best man, and Ruth Kehr was Elvina's maid of honor.

I served a lunch afterwards of chicken sandwiches, cake, and some heart and Cupid shaped molds of ice cream that I ordered from Denver through Al Kehr's Chocolate Shop in Ogallala. My sister Ethel arranged for them to spend their brief honeymoon in a small cottage on the Patrick place. Afterwards they moved into a small house on a farm Arnold rented from Arch Searle.

We had a new Studebaker that summer, and we decided to take Ruth to Yellowstone to see the bears and animals. We also wanted to go see the Bell family again. They were living in Idaho at this time. It was a hot, dry summer that year, and we certainly enjoyed the cool of the mountains. Ruthie got to see lots of bears, and then we drove into Idaho to try and locate Gus and Mary Bell. As we drove into a little place to get some gas, Arelias said, "This looks like good cattle country."

I looked around and said, "But there aren't any cattle around."

Arelias parked by a gas pump and climbed out of the car as he said, " I'm going over there and ask that old timer why we haven't seen any cattle."

He walked across the street, and just then another car pulled up to the other gas pump beside us. Would you believe it was BELLS? They had a doctor and his wife from Georgia visiting them, and they were all headed for Yellowstone Park to camp and fish. Jim Bell looked across the street and said to his dad, "Who's that over there?"

Old Gus Bell exclaimed, "By grannies, that's Berry!" Well we all hugged and shook hands, and then we joined forces and returned to Yellowstone Park. We made camp together in the northwest corner the park, and had a great time fishing and visiting for several days. I remember so well seeing Jim Bell next morning frying pancakes for everyone over a camp fire.

We left for home a few days later, and went south toward Gordon Jewitt's ranch. Arelias hoped to see him again also, but we missed him. When we got to the ranch, Mrs. Jewitt said Gordon had just left with a pack horse to scout a way to drive their cattle out of the high country to market. Arelias felt we couldn't wait until Jewitt returned. He had told John we would be home, so we left and arrived next day.

Elaine McKeag Nielsen

GLAD TIMES; SAD TIMES

We rented an apartment in Ogallala during the winter of 1929-1930. Part of the time Mother and Dad lived there because Dad's health was failing a bit all of the time. He'd had several strokes by then. Patricks rented a nearby apartment so that Ethel could watch over our parents and put Della in high school in Ogallala for her senior year. Elvina was expecting a baby in February, and so she also stayed at our apartment the first part of that month.

Our first grandchild arrived February 18, 1930, in a complicated fashion. Elvina's doctor was called to Keystone to deliver a baby at the same time as Elvina went to the hospital. He called an old doctor in Ogallala who was really not practicing much any more to see to Elvina while he was in Keystone. (I was out at the ranch that day with a bad cold, and knew nothing of all this because we didn't have a phone then.) Elvina had very little confidence in the old doctor—-she scarcely knew him—-so she had Arnold call my sister Ethel to be on hand. Ethel was like Mother where births were concerned, and she had presided over several deliveries around Lemoyne.

It was a difficult birth because the babe came backwards. Well, that doctor didn't seem to know what to do. Ethel was never one to mince words, and she gave him some stern instructions about how to proceed—-and quickly. At last they delivered an eight and a half pound baby girl with dark hair. Elvina and Arnold named the baby "Elaine Devine".

1929 was a very dry year, and the farm crops mostly failed. Arnold had very little to show for a year of hard labor. Arelias talked to him when it came time to rent the farm for another year. Our calves had sold pretty well that fall, and Arelias wanted to invest in some land to set them up in ranching. However, he wanted Arnold to work for him a year first to learn about ranching. He told Arnold, "Son, you do what you think best, but a cow usually has a calf whether it rains or not."

Arnold decided to ranch, and when Elvina got out of the hospital they moved out to our place with the new baby to live in a small house we had moved into the home valley.

By that time we were all busy arranging a big celebration for March 21, 1930, Mother and Dad's Golden Wedding Anniversary. We planned a dinner at the Methodist Church dining room in Ogallala. All of the old friends and neighbors of former times were invited, as well as all of our families. It was quite a gathering that Friday when we sat down to dinner together. The Reverend Campbell from the Lemoyne church addressed the assembled group, and made much of what an inspiration Mother and Dad's life together must be to everyone. All nine of us children were on hand as well as thirty one grandchildren and six great grandchildren.

After dinner Rev. Campbell asked old timers to respond to "Joys and Sorrows of Wedded Life on a Homestead". There were several musical selections on the program. Della Patrick sang a solo, "I Have Grown So Used to You", and then a choral group sang, "Put On Your Old Gray Bonnet". After the benediction we all sang the old hymn, "Blest Be the Tie That Binds". Although Dad was unable to stand or walk much at this time, he was able to visit with everyone from his chair, and he and Mother seemed to enjoy the whole afternoon a lot. Dad was a long time member of Woodmen of the World, and they gave him and Mother a bouquet of rose buds in honor of the occasion.

Dad's condition worsened after that. He and Mother did not return to California. They stayed some of the time that summer with Bea in a house near Peterson's Pond on the old Holcomb place. Dad would sit and fish by the pond or just watch the ducks on it. Sometimes he amused himself by tossing crumbs out on the water to watch the ducklings scramble for them. In the fall they moved into the little house on the Patrick place to be near Ethel and Ad.

Della Patrick went away to college that fall in Missouri. She came home the following spring quite a grown up young lady. In July she insisted on going swimming even though she had a cold. Soon afterwards she developed pneumonia, and she died within a few days. I stayed with Mother and Dad at the little Patrick house during the funeral. It was a sad time.

After he graduated from high school in 1928 John went right to work on the ranch. He was always so handy with cars and machinery. Sometime in the early Twenties Arelias installed a Delco light plant there to light up the house instead of kerosene lamps. Whenever the batteries got low, the Delco came on to charge them up again. When the water began to come up everywhere it also came up in the cellar. Arelias would send John down to bucket the water out of the cellar so it wouldn't be on the light engine and batteries. John soon got tired of doing this chore over and over. He contrived a pump that he hooked up to the fan of the Delco. He ran a pipe up the stairs and out on to the ground so that when the Delco went on it pumped water out of the cellar on to the ground. Arelias was standing by the cellar looking at the whole arrangement just after John had put it together. He said to me, "Wonder what 'Splinter' (his nick name for John) is up to now." He had his pants tucked into his boots, and about that time the Delco went on and water poured out of the pipe and right into his boot. It must have been about this time Arelias said, "I believe one of these days I'd better build John a shop."

John drove a 1929 Ford roadster. He had a portable wind-up phonograph and quite a collection of records of popular tunes, and how he like to dance! Still, he worked hard, and like Arelias, he was a real hand on horseback. He soon began to take part in rodeos. I suppose I worried most about his love of airplanes, which were new to this country then. John wanted above all things to learn to fly one.

During the 'Thirties we opened the lake to the public and charged people a dollar to fish for an afternoon. It proved to be a lot of bother though, and not worth the headaches the public caused. Some people would go to great lengths to fish without paying the dollar. I remember one man who was out in the middle of the lake when I noticed him. He hadn't paid, and I hollered at him to come do so. He wasn't going to come, but he changed his mind when I fired a .22 shell along side his boat.

One man from Ogallala kept coming to fish. He always left one or more gates open along the trail. John was a young man by that time, and he cured the man of his bad habit. John buried a cross cut saw, notched edge up, in the road on a day when he knew the gate opener was coming. Just beyond the first gate, the culprit had four flat tires. He didn't do any fishing that day. After he fixed the four tires he headed back to town, again across the saw blade, and had four more. Soon after that we closed the lake to the public.

Elsie gave Arelias a barometer that had belonged to Henry Pope. Arelias studied it a lot and found it very useful in predicting weather changes. One day in March of 1931 the weather turned quite warm as it sometimes does in Nebraska. Arelias checked that barometer, and it was lower than he'd ever seen it before. Arnold and John were freighting cotton cake from Lemoyne to the ranch. It had been dry the summer before, and we were a bit short of hay. Arelias was going to feed the cotton cake to supplement the hay and old grass that spring. When they got back in the afternoon Arelias helped them unload and put the team in the barn. He told them to eat some supper and get in some fresh horses. He was sure it was going to storm.

Long before daybreak Arelias got up to check the weather. He found that heavy snow was falling, and the wind was coming up. He woke all of the men and sent Arnold and John east to gather cattle while he and Homer Bowden went south. Arnold and John got their territory gathered and the cows and calves home behind the grove of trees all right. The wind shifted to the north, and Arelias and Homer had a mighty tough time moving theirs against the wind into the grove. They all worked together and finally got that bunch in shelter. Then Homer, John, and Arnold built a fence in the storm across the open end of the grove to keep the cattle from drifting out again. Only after that did they come in to get dry and warm. It was an awful storm, but we only lost one calf, and many ranchers lost most of their herds in it.

Arelias took Arnold and Elvina around to look at land that was for sale, and eventually they decided on some in Arthur County. Arelias bought it, and they began to make a place to live on it. There was one nice wet meadow in a large valley that seemed the best place to have a house and barn located. The William Simons family lived in the east end of the valley, and it seemed good to have neighbors in sight. There was a pretty good frame house on the adjoining section, so they moved it into the valley and began to make it livable. Arelias and Arnold put down a well on top of a tall hill back of the house. They dug a deep hole beside it and lined it with cement to make a cistern for the well. Then they dug a ditch to pipe water from it into the house so Elvina would have water in the house. They also piped it to the barn and corrals for the livestock.

In May Elvina and Arnold were able to move in to their new home. Elvina was expecting another baby by then. In July she came to town to await its arrival. July 12 she had twin girls, both of them weighing over six pounds. They named them "Dorothy Edith" and "Dorinne Leona" after both grandmothers.

(John and Beulah Berry)

John went to Belle Fouche, South Dakota, for the Fourth of July Rodeo. On the way he stopped to visit Beulah Blakeney, a girl he'd been taking to dances and seeing quite a bit. (She was from Ogallala, and went to high school with Elvina.) Beulah was attending summer school at the Chadron State Teachers College to get her teacher's certificate. Blessed if they didn't take a notion to go to Spearfish and get married on July 2!

When the rodeo was over she went back to school and he came home. He did not tell us about it right away. Walt Haythorn had

attended the same rodeo, and after a while he mentioned to Arelias that he had read John and Beulah's names in the marriage license notices in the Spearfish newspaper. Arelias asked John at once what THAT was all about. John told him then that they were married. Arelias immediately said, "Any son of mine can bring his wife home." So they moved into the little house in our yard where Elvina and Arnold had lived so recently.

In the spring of 1932 at a family gathering, several of the men were shooting and what not. Dad was failing and had had more strokes, but he still wanted to take part so several of the men lifted him up to take a shot at some blue rocks. He aimed a gun with their help and broke one right on target. He killed his first wild turkey when he was eight, and shot his last blue rock when he was 78.

In June of 1932 Emma (Patrick) Burch agreed to drive Mrs. Adams to see a doctor in North Platte. Mother wasn't feeling very well, and we urged her to go along and see a doctor also. They left on a Thursday morning in Emma's car. Emma drove down the highway near the town of Hershey and found the road had recently been graded, and there was a ridge of gravel in the center. Because it was so dry the gravel grade was like a washboard. As Emma drove along one wheel caught in the gravel ridge and caused her to lose control of the car. It spun across the ridge into the path of an oncoming car. There was an awful wreck. Everyone in Emma's car was badly injured. They were all taken to the Platte Valley Hospital in North Platte.

On Friday, June 9, 1932, our mother died of head injuries. The next day Mrs. Adams died. Emma remained in the hospital for several weeks with a broken leg and pelvic injuries. When they told Dad that Mother was gone he demanded to see her. Dad was mostly confined to bed by that time, but Arrowsmith agreed to bring the body out to Patricks for Dad to see one last time. When the hearse arrived, three of his sons-in-law lifted Dad up to view Mother in her coffin. He gazed at her for several minutes, and then they took him away. After that his mind began to be confused, and his condition worsened in every way.

After the funeral we all gathered to sort Mother's things, and each of us took some thing to treasure and remember as hers. I brought home her nutmeg grater. We all agreed to let Kenneth have her gold wedding ring. He eventually gave it to Florence Scott, whom he married November 11, 1934. (Florence was teaching school in Lemoyne at the time.)

In September Dad died also. His last months were difficult. He was bed ridden, confused, and desolate for Mother. Death came as a blessed release for him. Still, we grieved. Our family had been so close for so long.

Life went on, though, as it always does. Elvina was so very busy with her three little ones. Arelias and I enjoyed them a lot. As Elaine got a little older, Arnold would sometimes bring her along and leave her with me while he worked with John and Arelias. (They often helped each other work cattle or put up hay.) Ruthie played with Elaine a lot, even though she was nearly five years older.

When Ruth started to school I rented a house in Ogallala and put her in school there. We usually came home to the ranch on weekends when the weather permitted. When Ruth was a third grader, Elvina was expecting another child. She came to town to stay with me just before it was due. On January 22, my brother Willard's birthday, she had another little girl. Such a beautiful baby! Arnold insisted she be named "Gail Elvina".

1934 was a good year for us in many ways, even though the times were hard in general. When he re-subscribed to The Texas Cattleman Magazine, Arelias wrote a letter to the editor that was reprinted in the June issue, 1934. He wrote,

"...Renew my subscription for five years. I do not want to miss a copy. It comes like a friend from home. I was raised in Texas. The Cattleman has more news of interest to the cattle raiser than any other paper I take. It keeps you posted on the range news from Texas to Montana. I well remember some of the ranches and cowmen and cow ponies spoken of in your paper. I well remember seeing Sam Graves cutting cattle on old 'Hub' at the Cowboy Reunion in Haskell, Texas, without a bridle on him. I think this was in 1893. I scan the death column with sorrow as I notice the passing of some old-time cowmen I have worked for or with."

With the letter he included a picture of some of the Flying X registered Hereford bulls. The editor also printed the picture with this caption beneath it:

"The Berry ranch in the Sand Hills country of Nebraska is north of the Platte River and is known as the "Flying X." He is a member of the executive committee of the Nebraska Stockgrowers Association. There is an abundance of grass for summer grazing and hay in the valleys for winter feeding. There are 7 flowing wells, 10 windmills and 2 lakes on this ranch. About 1,100 grade Hereford cattle are carried. Nothing but registered bulls have been used for the past twenty years."

I read it and marveled again at this Texan I married that day in the house on Lonergan Creek in 1906. We had lived a very full life in the time since. I was unusually thankful that fall when we gathered with the relatives for Thanksgiving dinner at Patricks. (We had all planned to go to Kurkowskis' but at the last minute when one of Letha and Ed's kids got the mumps, Ethel and Ad told everyone to come there.) Even though Mother and Dad had departed this world, still there were three generations of us Stansberys on hand that day. After dinner we took a picture of the whole crowd. Arelias and I each held one of 'Vina and Arnold's twins. Elvina held Gail, who was a curly haired toddler by then, and Elaine and Ruth stood with a whole group of the younger cousins in the front row. John and Beulah were both there and so many others of the young married couples. It was a glad time that helped to heal the recent sad days.

Thanksgiving 1934, at the Patricks'

THE END

Edith Berry playing her beloved fiddle

AFTERWARD

A.B. Berry died the following year, in 1935. Edith Berry turned over operation of the ranch to their son, John, and moved to Wyoming, where she lived for many years in a cabin in the Tensleep Canyon. Edith Berry later moved back to Nebraska, and passed away in 1986, at the age of 99.

Two of A.B. and Edith's children, John and Elvina, passed away in 1999. Their youngest, Ruth, lives in Sun Lakes, Arizona, with her husband, Stan Snyder.

Elvina's eldest daughter, Elaine Devine McKeag Nielsen, who wrote this book, also passed away in 1999.

W.P. and Elvina Stansbery's descendents today number in the hundreds.

About the Author

Elaine Nielsen was born on February 18, 1930. Her parents were Arnold and Elvina McKeag, ranchers near Arthur, Nebraska. She attended a country school through the eighth grade, and subsequently graduated from Ogallala High School in 1947. She then attended Ottawa University in Ottawa, Kansas. She married Gene Nielsen, an Ogallala rancher, in 1950. Together they raised five children. She was a regular contributor to the *Keith County News*, the *North Platte Telegraph* and *Western Outlook Magazine*, and also wrote articles for other publications, including *Persimmon Hill* (the official magazine of the Cowboy Hall of Fame). She won awards as an active member of the Nebraska Press Women and Nebraska Writers Guild. She authored a history of Ogallala entitled *Ogallala, A Century on the Trail*, which was published in 1984. She edited a book for Hershey (Nebraska)'s Centennial. She was a longtime member of the Keith County Historical society, the Ogallala Regional Arts Council, and the Keith County Republican Party, often as an officer. She was an organist and active member of St. Luke's Catholic Church in Ogallala. She died of cancer on February 17, 1999.

CPSIA information can be obtained
at www.ICGtesting.com
Printed in the USA
BVHW041100120423
662066BV00001B/80

9 798215 648285